Praise for *Next Generation Assessment*

"Measuring (and, therefore, teaching) what really matte[...] demands that we capture students' readiness to apply kno[...] non-routine, real-world tasks. Such assessments push t[...] expertise; they also confront deep-seated cultural norms[...] leading scholars offer both state-of-the-art expertise an[...] [...]viding much-needed guidance to those developing, advocating for, adopting, implementing, and learning from measures that really matter."

—Jeannie Oakes, Director, Educational Opportunity and Scholarship, Ford Foundation

"*Next Generation Assessment* promotes a forward-thinking, proactive approach to evaluating student learning in ways that respect students as individual learners and respect educators as the professionals they are. Darling-Hammond and colleagues masterfully describe how performance assessments can become a meaningful part of the crucial teaching and learning process, rather than replacing it. As educators fight to get rid of low-quality tests that help our kids learn to fill in bubbles, this book provides a promising alternative that involves educators in the development and scoring of performance assessments in ways that are beneficial to them and to their students. Educators have been clamoring for common-sense solutions and this work delivers!"

—Dennis Van Roekel, President, National Education Association

"*Next Generation Assessment* helps readers think strategically about accountability and assessment in America's public schools and understand how performance-based approaches—instead of rote memorization—can allow schools to support both deeper learning and higher standards. This is the way students can develop the skills and knowledge they need for life, citizenship, college, and career. In this important volume, Linda Darling-Hammond and colleagues show how much is known about a better path forward on testing and accountability, if only we are willing to take it."

—Randi Weingarten, President, American Federation of Teachers

"This book sheds new light on how educational testing policies are improving or hindering the measurement of students' abilities to think and learn in ways that will assure their success. Linda Darling-Hammond and colleagues build a case for educational policy and decision makers to provide the time and resources needed to shift to balanced performance assessment, moving way beyond test scores, toward more authentic teaching and learning."

—Gail Connelly, Executive Director, National Association of
Elementary School Principals

"This work comes at a critical time as education leaders in all fifty states grapple with how to move to a system of performance assessments that reflects the more rigorous deeper learning outcomes they are seeking. Pointing to current policies and practice, this book is an excellent guide directing practitioners and policymakers on how to transition to an assessment system that genuinely shapes, informs, and improves learning for all students and teachers."

—Governor Bob Wise, President, Alliance for Excellent Education;
author of *Raising the Grade*

Next Generation Assessment

Moving Beyond the Bubble Test to Support 21st Century Learning

Linda Darling-Hammond
in collaboration with

Jamal Abedi • Frank Adamson • Jillian Chingos •
David T. Conley • Beverly Falk • Ann Jaquith • Stuart
Kahl • Suzanne Lane • William Montague • John Olson •
Margaret Owens • Raymond Pecheone • Lawrence O. Picus •
Ed Roeber • Brian Stecher • Thomas Toch • Barry Topol

JB JOSSEY-BASS™
A Wiley Brand

Published by Jossey-Bass
A Wiley Brand
One Montgomery Street, Suite 1200, San Francisco, CA 94104-4594—www.josseybass.com

Jossey-Bass books and products are available through most bookstores. To contact Jossey-Bass directly call our Customer Care Department within the U.S. at 800-956-7739, outside the U.S. at 317-572-3986, or fax 317-572-4002.

Wiley publishes in a variety of print and electronic formats and by print-on-demand. Some material included with standard print versions of this book may not be included in e-books or in print-on-demand. If this book refers to media such as a CD or DVD that is not included in the version you purchased, you may download this material at http://booksupport.wiley.com. For more information about Wiley products, visit www.wiley.com.

Library of Congress Cataloging-in-Publication Data has been applied for and is on file with the Library of Congress.

ISBN 978-1-118-45617-0 (pbk.)
ISBN 978-1-118-92812-7 (ebk.)
ISBN 978-1-118-92813-4 (ebk.)

Printed in the United States of America
FIRST EDITION
PB Printing   10 9 8 7 6 5 4 3 2 1

CONTENTS

Acknowledgments   vi

The Authors   vii

1 Beyond the Bubble Test: How Performance
Assessment Can Support Deeper Learning   1

2 Defining Performance Assessment   15

3 Experiences with Performance Assessment in
the United States and Abroad   31

4 How Performance Assessment Can Support Student
and Teacher Learning   43

5 Meeting the Challenges of Performance
Assessments   57

6 Making High-Quality Assessment Affordable   75

7 Building Systems of Assessment   87

8 Conclusion   107

Notes   113

Index   125

ACKNOWLEDGMENTS

This book assembles the key insights from a more comprehensive volume, published separately by Jossey-Bass—*Beyond the Bubble Test: How Performance Assessment Supports 21st Century Teaching and Learning*—that summarizes research and lessons learned regarding the development, implementation, and consequences of performance assessments. The project examines experiences with and lessons from large-scale performance assessment in the United States and abroad, including technical advances, feasibility issues, policy implications, uses with English Language Learners, and costs.

The work was funded by the Ford Foundation, Hewlett Foundation, Nellie Mae Educational Foundation, and Sandler Foundation and guided by an advisory board of education researchers, practitioners, and policy analysts, ably chaired by Richard Shavelson. The board shaped specifications for commissioned papers that became some of these chapters and reviewed these papers on their completion. We are grateful to these funders and to advisory board members Eva Baker, Christopher Cross, Nicholas Donahue, Michael Feuer, Edward Haertel, Jack Jennings, Peter McWalters, Lorrie Shepard, Guillermo Solano-Flores, Brenda Welburn, and Gene Wilhoit for their support and wisdom.

The contributors to this book thank all the educators and other innovators over many years who have devoted hundreds of thousands of hours to developing and implementing thoughtful curriculum and assessments that support students and teachers in their learning.

We also thank Sonya Keller for her helpful and thorough editorial assistance and Samantha Brown for her help securing permissions for the entries in this book. Early versions of these papers were ably ushered into production by Barbara McKenna. Without their efforts, this project would not have come to fruition.

THE AUTHORS

Jamal Abedi, professor of education at the University of California, Davis, specializes in educational and psychological assessments. His research focus is testing for English language learners and issues concerning the technical characteristics and interpretations of these assessments. From 2010 to the present, Abedi has served as a member of the Technical Advisory Committee of the SMARTER Balanced Assessment Consortium. Before then, he served on the expert panel of the US Department of Education's LEP Partnership and he was founder and chair of AERA's Special Interest Group on Inclusion and Accommodation in Large-Scale Assessment. In 2008, the California Educational Research Association gave him its Lifetime Achievement Award. Abedi received his PhD from Vanderbilt University.

Frank Adamson, a policy and research analyst at the Stanford Center for Opportunity Policy in Education (SCOPE), currently focuses on the adoption of assessments of deeper learning and twenty-first-century skills at the state, national, and international levels. He also conducts research on educational equity and opportunities to learn and has published on teacher salary differences within labor markets in New York and California. Prior to joining SCOPE, Adamson worked at AIR and SRI International designing assessments, evaluating US education initiatives, and developing international indicators for the OECD and UNESCO. He received an MA in sociology and a PhD in international comparative education from Stanford University.

Jillian Chingos (previously Jillian Hamma) is currently a sixth-grade teacher at Alpha: Blanca Alvarado Middle School in San Jose, California.

Chingos attended Dartmouth College, where she majored in English, minored in public policy, and received her teaching credential. She previously worked at the Stanford Center for Assessment, Learning, and Equity, developing and researching performance assessments.

David T. Conley is professor of educational policy and leadership and founder and director of the Center for Educational Policy Research (CEPR) at the University of Oregon. He is also the founder, chief executive officer, and chief strategy officer of the Educational Policy Improvement Center and president of CCR Consulting Group, both in Eugene and Portland, Oregon. Through these organizations, he conducts research on a range of topics related to college readiness and other key policy issues with funding provided by grants and contracts from a range of national organizations, states, school districts, and school networks. His line of inquiry focuses on what it takes for students to succeed in postsecondary education. His latest publication, *Getting Ready for College, Careers, and the Common Core*, was recently published by Jossey-Bass (for more information, see www.collegecareerready.com).

Linda Darling-Hammond is Charles E. Ducommun professor of education and faculty director of the Stanford Center for Opportunity Policy in Education at Stanford University. Darling-Hammond is a former president of the American Educational Research Association and a member of the National Academy of Education. Her research and policy work focus on issues of educational equity, teaching quality, school reform, and performance assessment. In 2008, she served as director of President Obama's education policy transition team. Her book *The Flat World and Education: How America's Commitment to Equity Will Determine Our Future* received the coveted Grawemeyer Award in 2012. Her most recent book is *Getting Teacher Evaluation Right: What Really Matters for Effectiveness and Improvement* (2013).

Beverly Falk is professor and director of the graduate programs in early childhood education at the School of Education, City College of New York. Her areas of expertise include early childhood education, early literacy, performance assessment, school change, teacher education, and teacher research. She has served in a variety of educational roles: classroom teacher; school founder and director; district administrator; and consultant, fellow, and leader in schools, districts, states, and national organizations. Currently she is editor of the *New Educator* and senior scholar at the Stanford Center for Assessment, Learning and Equity. Falk received her EdD from Teachers College, Columbia University.

Ann Jaquith is associate director at Stanford Center for Opportunity Policy in Education. She has worked on a variety of performance assessment projects undertaken to reform schools in New York, Ohio, and California. As a former teacher and administrator, her expertise is in building the instructional and leadership capacity needed to use performance assessments to improve instruction and student learning. Her research interests include studying how instructional capacity gets built at different levels of the system and examining the practices professional development providers use that change instruction and improve student learning. She received her PhD in curriculum and teacher education from Stanford University.

Stuart Kahl is founding principal and CEO of Measured Progress as Advanced Systems in Measurement and Evaluation. A former elementary and secondary teacher, he worked for the Education Commission of the States, the University of Colorado, and RMC Research Corporation. A frequent speaker at industry conferences, Kahl also serves as a technical consultant to various education agencies. He has been recognized for his work in the areas of standard setting for non-multiple-choice instruments and the alignment of curriculum and assessment. Kahl received his PhD from the University of Colorado.

Suzanne Lane is professor at the University of Pittsburgh. Her recent research focuses on the implications for the next generation of assessments based on the lessons from classroom instruction and achievement in the 1990s, the assessment of twenty-first-century thinking skills, and the interplay among a theory of action, validity, and consequences. Lane has been the president of the National Council on Measurement in Education (2003–2004) and vice president of Division D of the American Educational Research Association (2002–2003). She received a PhD in research methodology, measurement, and statistics from the University of Arizona.

William Montague is a student at the University of Virginia School of Law. He began his career as a high school English teacher in Roanoke Rapids,

North Carolina, as a member of Teach For America. He went on to work for Independent Education, an association of independent schools in the Washington, DC, area. While there, he collaborated on a number of projects with the organization's executive director, Thomas Toch, a long-time education writer and policy analyst. Montague received his BA from the University of Virginia, where he majored in economics and history.

John Olson is senior partner of Assessment Solutions Group (ASG), which he cofounded in 2008. He is also president of the consulting business he founded in 2006, Olson Educational Measurement and Assessment Services, which provides technical assistance and support to states, school districts, federal bodies, testing companies, researchers, and others. He has more than thirty years of experience managing and consulting on a variety of measurement and statistical issues for international, national, state, and local assessment programs through his work at Harcourt Assessment, the Council for Chief State School Officers, the American Institutes for Research, and the Education Statistics Services Institute. He served in a number of leadership roles for the National Assessment of Educational Progress at the Educational Testing Service. Olson holds a PhD in educational statistics and measurement from the University of Nebraska–Lincoln.

Margaret Owens is currently a teacher at Mission High School in San Francisco. She earned her teaching credential and MA from Stanford University. Her studies focused on new pedagogical strategies, such as complex instruction, that bring more collaboration and engagement to students historically alienated in mathematics. Prior to her teaching career, she studied political science at Stanford with a focus on American education.

Raymond Pecheone is professor of practice at Stanford University and the founder and executive director of the Stanford Center for Assessment Learning, and Equity (SCALE). Under Pecheone, SCALE focuses on the development of performance assessments and performance-based systems for students, teachers, and administrators at the school, district, and state levels. Prior to launching SCALE, Pecheone was the bureau chief for curriculum, research, and assessment in the Connecticut State Department of Education; codirector of the first Assessment Development Lab for the

National Board for Professional Teaching Standards; and project director to support the redesign of the New York State Regents. Most recently, Pecheone and SCALE are developing the performance assessment specifications and tasks for the Smarter Balanced national assessment system. He received his PhD from the University of Connecticut in measurement and evaluation.

Lawrence O. Picus is vice dean for faculty affairs and professor at the Rossier School of Education, University of Southern California. He is an expert in the area of public financing of schools, equity and adequacy of school funding, school business administration, education policy, linking school resources to student performance, and resource allocation in schools. His current research interests focus on adequacy and equity in school finance, as well as efficiency and productivity in the provision of educational programs for PreK–12 children. Picus is past president of the Association for Education Finance and Policy, has served on the EdSource board of directors for twelve years, and has consulted extensively on school finance issues in more than twenty states. He earned a PhD in public policy analysis from the RAND Graduate School, an MA in social science from the University of Chicago, and a BA in economics from Reed College.

Ed Roeber is a consultant at Assessment Solutions Group (ASG). He has served as state assessment director in the Michigan Department of Education, director of student assessment programs for the Council for Chief State School Officers, vice president of Measured Progress, and adjunct professor at Michigan State University. For ASG and the other organizations, he advises states and other organizations on student assessment–related programs and functions. Currently he is a consultant on student assessment to several organizations (Michigan Assessment Consortium, Michigan State University, and Wisconsin Center for Educational Research/University of Wisconsin). He has written extensively about educational assessment, consulted with a number of agencies and organizations, and spoken frequently about student assessment. He has a PhD in educational measurement from the University of Michigan.

Brian Stecher is a senior social scientist and associate director of RAND Education and professor at the Pardee RAND Graduate School. His research focuses on measuring educational quality and evaluating education reforms, with an emphasis on assessment and accountability systems. During his more than twenty years at RAND, he has directed prominent national and state evaluations of No Child Left Behind, mathematics and science systemic reforms, and class size reduction. His measurement-related expertise includes test development, test validation, and the use of assessments for school improvement. Stecher has served on expert panels relating to standards, assessments, and accountability for the National Academies and is currently a member of the Board on Testing and Assessment. He received his PhD from the University of California, Los Angeles.

Thomas Toch is senior managing partner for public policy engagement at the Carnegie Foundation. He also serves as director of the Carnegie Foundation's Washington, DC, office. He is a founder and former codirector of the think tank Education Sector and a former guest scholar at the Brookings Institution, and he has taught at the Harvard Graduate School of Education. He helped launch *Education Week* in the 1980s. He spent a decade as the senior education correspondent at *US News and World Report* and has contributed to the *Atlantic*, the *New York Times,* and other national publications. His work has twice been nominated for National Magazine Awards. He is the author of two books on American education, *In the Name of Excellence* (Oxford University Press) and *High Schools on a Human Scale* (Beacon Press).

Barry Topol is managing partner of Assessment Solutions Group (ASG). He leads ASG in providing assessment cost, management, and state accountability systems analysis and consulting to states, universities, and other nonprofit institutions. Since forming ASG in 2009, Topol and ASG have worked with a number of states and the Partnership for Assessment of Readiness for College and Careers, and Smarter Balanced Assessment Consortium to assist them in designing their assessment and accountability systems to be more effective and efficient. Topol designed ASG's assessment cost model, the only model in the industry that can be used to determine the appropriate price for any assessment. Topol has a BA in economics from UCLA and an MBA from the Anderson School of Management at UCLA.

chapter 1

Beyond the Bubble Test
How Performance Assessment Can Support Deeper Learning

*I am calling on our nation's Governors and state education
chiefs to develop standards and assessments that don't simply
measure whether students can fill in a bubble on a test, but
whether they possess 21st century skills like problem-solving
and critical thinking, entrepreneurship and creativity.*
                        President Barack Obama, March 2009

Reform of educational standards and assessments has been a constant theme in nations around the globe. As part of an effort to keep up with countries that appear to be galloping ever further ahead educationally, US governors and chief state school officers recently issued a set of Common Core State Standards that aim to outline internationally benchmarked concepts and skills needed for success in today's and tomorrow's world.[1] The standards, which intend to create "fewer, higher, and deeper" curriculum goals, are meant to ensure that students are college and career ready.

Changes in teaching and testing are profoundly implicated by this goal. Genuine readiness for college and twenty-first-century careers, as well as participation in today's democratic society, requires, as President Obama has noted, much more than "bubbling in" on a test. Students need to be able to find, evaluate, synthesize, and use knowledge in new contexts, frame and solve nonroutine problems, and produce research findings and solutions. It also requires students to acquire well-developed thinking, problem-solving, design, and communication skills.

These are the so-called twenty-first-century skills that reformers around the world have been urging schools to pursue for decades—skills that are increasingly in demand in a complex, technologically connected, and fast-changing world. As research by economists Frank Levy and Richard Murnane shows, the routine skills used in factory jobs that once fueled an industrial economy have declined sharply in demand as they are computerized, outsourced, or made extinct by the changing nature of work. The skills in greatest demand now are the nonroutine interactive skills that are important for collaborative invention and problem solving. (See figure 1.1.)

In part, this is because knowledge is expanding at a breathtaking pace. Researchers at the University of California, Berkeley estimated that from

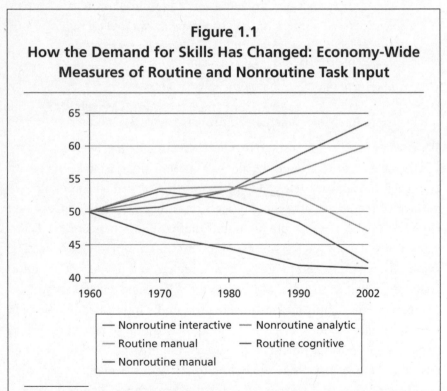

Figure 1.1
How the Demand for Skills Has Changed: Economy-Wide Measures of Routine and Nonroutine Task Input

Legend:
— Nonroutine interactive — Nonroutine analytic
— Routine manual — Routine cognitive
— Nonroutine manual

Source: Murnane, R., & Levy, F. (1996). *Teaching the new basic skills: Principles for educating children to thrive in a changing economy.* New York, NY: Free Press.

1999 to 2002, the amount of new information produced in the world exceeded the amount produced in the entire history of the world previously.[2] The amount of new technical information was doubling every two years at that time. It is now doubling annually.[3]

As a consequence, a successful education can no longer be organized by dividing a set of facts into the twelve years of schooling to be doled out bit by bit each year. Instead, schools must teach disciplinary knowledge in ways that also help students learn how to learn, so that they can use their knowledge in new situations and manage the demands of changing information, technologies, jobs, and social conditions.

These concerns have driven educational reforms in nations around the globe. For example, as Singapore prepared to overhaul its assessment system, its education minister at the time, Tharman Shanmugaratnam, noted, "[We need] less dependence on rote learning, repetitive tests and a 'one size fits all' type of instruction, and more on engaged learning, discovery through experiences, differentiated teaching, the learning of life-long skills, and the building of character, so that students can . . . develop the attributes, mindsets, character and values for future success."[4]

Whether the context is the changing nature of work, international competitiveness, or, most recently, calls for common standards, the premium today is not merely on students' acquiring information but on recognizing what kind of information matters, why it matters, and how to combine it with other information.[5] Remembering pieces of knowledge is no longer the highest priority for learning; what students can *do* with knowledge is what counts.

THE INFLUENCE OF TESTING ON LEARNING

During the 1990s, the advent of standards-based reform intended to move the education system toward twenty-first-century skills led many states and districts to develop systems that included open-ended assessments reflecting central ideas and performances in the disciplines.[6] These products—essays, mathematics tasks, research papers, scientific investigations, literary analyses, artistic exhibitions—were scored by teachers trained to evaluate the responses reliably. Studies found that these assignments improved the quality of instruction in states ranging from

California to Kentucky, Maine, Maryland, Vermont, and Washington[7] and improved achievement on both traditional standardized tests and more complex performance measures.[8]

However, performance assessments encountered rocky shoals in the United States as a function of implementation challenges, scoring costs, and conflicts with the requirements of No Child Left Behind (NCLB), the federal education law launched in 2002.[9] While NCLB introduced laudable goals for improving and equalizing school achievement, its approach to test-based accountability ultimately reduced the quality of assessments used by nearly all states.

Many states discontinued the assessments they had developed in the 1990s that required writing, research, and extended problem solving and replaced them with multiple-choice and short-answer tests. States abandoned performance assessments in part because of constraints placed on the types of tests approved by the US Department of Education as it reviewed state plans following NCLB passage, despite language supporting complex assessments in the law.

In addition, states had to adjust to strict NCLB testing time lines and a dramatic increase in costs with the law's requirement for every-child, every-year testing. Together these forces led to tests that rely heavily on multiple-choice questions that can be scored rapidly and inexpensively by machine. By their very nature, such tests are not well suited to judging students' ability to express points of view, marshal evidence, and display other advanced skills.

The General Accountability Office (GAO), the research branch of the US Congress, reported in 2009 that states' reliance on multiple-choice testing increased sharply in the NCLB era to achieve inexpensive scoring within tight time frames. Meanwhile, state education officials "reported facing trade-offs between efforts to assess highly complex content and to accommodate cost and time pressures."[10]

Indeed, a 2012 study by the RAND Corporation found that fewer than 2 percent of mathematics items and only about 20 percent of English language arts items on current state tests measure higher-order skills.[11] These skills, such as the abilities to analyze, synthesize, compare, connect, critique, hypothesize, prove, or explain ideas, are, in testing parlance, those represented at depth of knowledge levels 3 and 4 in the Webb taxonomy that classifies cognitive demand.[12] Levels 1 and 2 represent lower-level skills of recall, recognition, and use of routine procedures.

This study, which echoes the findings of other research,[13] is particularly worrisome, since these states were selected because their standards were viewed as especially rigorous. The RAND study found that the level of cognitive demand was severely constrained by the dominance of multiple-choice questions, which are rarely able to measure higher-order skills. Thus, the ambitious expectations found in state standards documents are frequently left unmeasured.

Assessment expert Lorrie Shepard and others have found that when educators teach directly to the content and format of specific high-stakes tests, students are frequently unable to transfer their knowledge to items that test that knowledge in different ways.[14] Furthermore, students' ability to answer multiple-choice questions does not mean they have the ability to answer the same questions in open-ended form. Indeed, their scores often drop precipitously when answers are not provided for them and they do not have the option to guess. Thus, a focus on multiple-choice testing gives false assurances about what students know and are able to do,[15] not only on other tests, but, more important, in the real world.

As Brian Stecher has noted, multiple-choice tests do not reflect the nature of performance in the real world, which rarely presents people with structured choices.[16] With the possible exception of a few game shows, we demonstrate our ability in the real world by applying knowledge and skills in settings where there are no predetermined options. A person balances her checkbook; buys ingredients and cooks a meal; reads an article in the newspaper and frames an opinion of the argument; assesses a customer's worthiness for a mortgage; interviews a patient, orders tests, and diagnoses the nature of this person's disease; and so on. Even in the context of school, the typical learning activity involves a mix of skills and culminates in a complex performance: a persuasive letter, a group project, a research paper, a first down, a band recital, a piece of art. Rarely does a citizen or a student have to choose among four distinct alternatives.

This would not be a major problem if tests were not used for more and more high-stakes decisions. Currently federal, state, and local governments have created policies that use test scores to determine student promotion from grade to grade, program placements, and graduation;

teacher tenure, continuation, and compensation; and school rewards and sanctions, including loss of funds and closure.

A long line of research has shown that—for good or ill—tests used for decision-making purposes can drive curriculum and instruction in ways that mimic both the content and the format of tests.[17] Because schools tend to teach what is tested, the expansion of multiple-choice measures of simple skills into curriculum and extensive test preparation activities has especially narrowed the opportunities of lower-achieving students to attain the higher standards that NCLB sought for them. It has also placed a glass ceiling over more advanced students, who are unable to demonstrate the depth and breadth of their abilities on such exams. The tests have discouraged teachers from teaching more challenging skills by having students conduct experiments, make oral presentations, write extensively, and do other sorts of intellectually challenging activities that pique students' interest in learning at the same time.[18]

This is why a growing number of educators and policymakers have argued that new assessments are needed. For example, Achieve, a national organization of governors, business leaders, and education leaders, has called for a broader view of assessment: "States . . . will need to move beyond large-scale assessments because, as critical as they are, they cannot measure everything that matters in a young person's education. The ability to make effective oral arguments and conduct significant research projects are considered essential skills by both employers and postsecondary educators, but these skills are very difficult to assess on a paper-and pencil test."[19]

The NCLB school accountability model and the standardized testing that undergirds it have not catalyzed the law's pursuit of twenty-first-century skills for all students. At best they have established an academic floor for the nation's students, even though the law itself calls for schools to teach students to higher standards. And while many struggling students need large doses of reading and math to catch up, there's ample research revealing that sophisticated reading skills and the necessary vocabulary for comprehension are best learned in the context of history, science, and other subjects.[20] Yet as the Center on Education Policy has documented, NCLB has narrowed the curriculum for many students, encouraging teachers to focus not only on the content but also the format of the tests at the expense of other essential kinds of learning.[21]

As one teacher noted in a national survey:

> Before [our state test] I was a better teacher. I was exposing my children to a wide range of science and social studies experiences. I taught using themes that really immersed the children into learning about a topic using their reading, writing, math, and technology skills. Now I'm basically afraid to NOT teach to the test. I know that the way I was teaching was building a better foundation for my kids, as well as a love of learning.

Another, echoing the findings of researchers, observed:

> I have seen more students who can pass the [state test] but cannot apply those skills to anything if it's not in the test format. I have students who can do the test but can't look up words in a dictionary and understand the different meanings. . . . As for higher quality teaching, I'm not sure I would call it that. Because of the pressure for passing scores, more and more time is spent practicing the test and putting everything in [the test] format.[22]

A third raised the concern that many experts have pointed to—pressure to speed through the topics that might be tested in a curriculum that is a mile wide and an inch deep:

> I believe that the [state test] is pushing students and teachers to rush through curriculum much too quickly. Rather than focusing on getting students to understand a concept fully in math, we must rush through all the subjects so we are prepared to take the test in March. This creates a surface knowledge or many times very little knowledge in a lot of areas. I would rather spend a month on one concept and see my students studying in an in-depth manner.[23]

In contrast, international surveys have shown that higher-scoring countries in mathematics and science teach fewer concepts each year but teach them more deeply than in the United States, so that students have a stronger foundation to support higher-order learning in the upper grades.[24] Ironically, states that test more topics in a grade level may encourage more superficial coverage, leading to less solid learning.

It is therefore not surprising that while student scores have risen sharply on the state tests used for accountability purposes under NCLB, scores have not increased commensurately on tests that gauge students' ability to apply knowledge to novel problems, such as the Program for International Student Assessment (PISA). US scores on PISA changed little between 2000 and 2012. After nearly a decade of test-based accountability, in 2012 the United States ranked thirty-second among member countries of the Organization for Economic Cooperation and Development in mathematics, twenty-third in science, and twenty-first in reading. Furthermore, US students scored lowest on the problem-solving tasks.[25]

PISA differs from most tests in the United States, in that most items call on students to write their own answers to questions that require weighing and balancing evidence, evaluating ideas, finding and manipulating information to answer complex questions, and solving problems. These kinds of items resemble the tests commonly used in other countries, which routinely use extended essay questions and complex open-ended problems to evaluate knowledge. Students in many high-achieving nations also have to design and complete science investigations, technology solutions, and research projects as part of their examinations, ensuring their readiness for college-level work.

By contrast, with a few exceptions, testing in most US states has been less focused on higher-order skills during the NCLB era than it was in the 1990s, even though it has increasingly functioned as a primary influence on curriculum and classroom instruction. Thus, while students in high-achieving nations are engaged in the kind of learning aimed at preparing to succeed in college and in the modern workplace, students in the United States have been drilling for multiple-choice tests that encourage recognition of simple right answers rather than the production of ideas.

EMERGING OPPORTUNITIES FOR BETTER ASSESSMENT

In addition to the new Common Core State Standards (CCSS) in English language arts and mathematics, a consortium of states has developed a set of Next Generation Science Standards (NGSS) that also aim for more intellectually ambitious learning and teaching. These new standards offer an opportunity to address the fundamental misalignment between our aspirations for students and the assessments we use to measure whether they are achieving those goals. The United States has a chance to create a new generation of assessments that build on NCLB's commitment to improve the education of traditionally underserved groups of students, while measuring a wider range of skills and expanding instruction to include the teaching of such skills.

To match international standards, new assessments will need to rely more heavily on what testing experts call performance measures—tasks requiring students to craft their own responses rather than merely selecting multiple-choice answers. Researchers argue that by tapping into students' advanced thinking skills and abilities to explain their reasoning, performance assessments yield a more complete picture of students' strengths and weaknesses. And by giving teachers a role in scoring essays and other performance measures, the way the Advanced Placement and International Baccalaureate programs do today, performance-oriented assessments encourage teachers to teach the skills measured by the assessments and help teachers learn how to do so. Such measures would, in other words, focus attention more directly on the improvement of classroom instruction than NCLB has done.

The recently released report of the Gordon Commission (2013), sponsored by the Educational Testing Service and written by the nation's leading experts in curriculum, teaching, and assessment, described the most critical objectives this way:[26]

> To be helpful in achieving the learning goals laid out in the Common Core, assessments must fully represent the competencies that the increasingly complex and changing world demands. The best assessments can accelerate the acquisition of these competencies if they guide the actions of teachers and enable students to gauge their progress. To do so, the tasks

and activities in the assessments must be models worthy of the attention and energy of teachers and students. The Commission calls on policy makers at all levels to actively promote this badly needed transformation in current assessment practice. . . . The assessment systems [must] be robust enough to drive the instructional changes required to meet the standards . . . and provide evidence of student learning useful to teachers.

At least a modest step in this direction is intended by the two multistate consortia creating assessments to evaluate the CCSS—the Partnership for Assessing Readiness for College and Careers (PARCC) and the Smarter Balanced Assessment Consortium (SBAC). PARCC and SBAC assessments, to be launched in 2014–2015, will increase the use of constructed response items and performance tasks.

The plans for the new consortia assessments suggest they will increase cognitive demand, offering more tasks that require students to analyze, critique, evaluate, and apply knowledge. An analysis of the Content Specifications for the Smarter Balanced Assessment Consortium found, for example, that 68 percent of the assessment targets in English language arts and 70 percent of those in mathematics intend to tap these higher-level skills (Herman & Linn, 2013).[27] The sample tasks released by the two consortia include performance tasks that encourage instruction aimed at helping students acquire and use knowledge in more complex ways. (See exhibits 1.1 and 1.2.)

Exhibit 1.1   Mathematics Performance Tasks

SBAC Sixth-Grade Task: Planning a Field Trip

Classroom Activity: The teacher introduces the topic and activates students' prior knowledge of planning field trips by:

- Leading students in a whole class discussion about where they have previously been on field trips or other outings, with their school, youth group, or family.

- Creating a chart showing the class's preferences by having students' first list and then vote on the places they would most like to go on a field trip, followed by whole class discussion on the top choices.

  Student Task: Individual students:

- Recommend where their class should go on a field trip, based on their analysis of the class vote.
- Determine the per-student cost of going on a field trip to three different locations, based on a chart showing the distance and entrance fees for each option, plus formula for bus charges.
- Use information from the cost chart to evaluate a hypothetical student's recommendation about going to the zoo.
- Write a note to their teacher recommending and justifying which field trip the class should take, based on an analysis of all available information.

PARCC High School Task: Golf Balls in Water

Part A: Students analyze data from an experiment involving the effect on the water level of adding golf balls to a glass of water in which they:

- Explore approximately linear relationships by identifying the average rate of change.
- Use a symbolic representation to model the relationship.

  Part B: Students suggest modifications to the experiment to increase the rate of change.
  Part C: Students interpret linear functions using both parameters by examining how results change when a glass with a smaller radius is used by:

- Explaining how the *y*-intercepts of two graphs will be different.
- Explaining how the rate of change differs between two experiments.
- Using a table, equation, or other representation to justify how many golf balls should be used.

Source: Herman, J. L., & Linn, R. L. (2013). *On the road to assessing deeper learning: The status of Smarter Balanced and PARCC assessment consortia* (CRESST Report No. 823). Los Angeles: University of California, National Center for Research on Evaluation, Standards, and Student Testing. See also http://ccsstoolbox.agilemind.com/parcc/about_highschool_3834.html and http://www.smarterbalanced.org/wordpress/wp-content/uploads/2012/09/performance-tasks/fieldtrip.pdf.

Exhibit 1.2   English Language Arts Performance Tasks

PARCC Seventh-Grade Task: Evaluating Amelia Earhart's Life

Summary Essay: Using textual evidence from the *Biography of Amelia Earhart*, students write an essay to summarize and explain the challenges Amelia Earhart faced throughout her life.

   Reading/Pre-Writing: After reading *Earhart's Final Resting Place Believed Found*, students:

- Use textual evidence to determine which of three given claims about Earhart and her navigator, Noonan, is the most relevant to the reading.
- Select two facts from the text to support the claim selected.

   Analytic Essay: Students:

- Read a third text called *Amelia Earhart's Life and Disappearance*.
- Analyze the evidence presented in all three texts concerning Amelia Earhart's bravery.
- Write an essay, using textual evidence, analyzing the strength of the arguments presented about Amelia Earhart's bravery in at least two of the texts.

SBAC Eleventh-Grade Task: Nuclear Power—Friend or Foe?

Classroom Activity: Using stimuli such as a chart and photos, the teacher prepares students for Part 1 of the assessment by leading students in a discussion of the use of nuclear power. Through discussion:

- Students share prior knowledge about nuclear power.
- Students discuss the use and controversies involving nuclear power.

   Part 1: Students complete reading and pre-writing activities in which they:

- Read and take notes on a series of Internet sources about the pros and cons of nuclear power.
- Respond to two constructed-response questions that ask students to analyze and evaluate the credibility of the arguments in favor and in opposition to nuclear power.

   Part 2: Students individually compose a full-length, argumentative report for their congressperson in which they use textual evidence to justify the position they take pro or con on whether a nuclear power plant should be built in their state.

Source: Herman & Linn (2013). See also http://www.parcconline.org/samples/english-language
-artsliteracy/grade-7-elaliteracy. http://www.smarterbalanced.org/wordpress/wp-content/uploads
/2012/09/performance-tasks/nuclear.pdf

Even these more ambitious assessment tasks, each conducted in a one- or two-day session, will not measure all of the CCSS skills—such as extended writing and research, oral communications, collaboration, and uses of technology for investigation, modeling solutions to complex problems, and multimedia presentation. Furthermore, as shown in figure 1.2, the CCSC represent only a subset of the full range of college- and career-readiness expectations, including knowledge and skills in content areas beyond English language arts and math, traits such as resourcefulness and perseverance, key learning skills and cognitive strategies, and transition knowledge and skills.

These skills are evaluated in a growing number of countries, which require students to design and conduct complex projects that may take many days or weeks to complete and require considerable student planning, perseverance, and problem solving. The products of this work are evaluated by teachers, using a moderation process that trains them to score reliably, and are included in examination results.

Some states and districts, such as those belonging to the Innovation Lab Network, coordinated by the Council for Chief State School Officers, plan to introduce even more extensive performance assessments to complement the consortium tests. These may include longer-term tasks that require students to undertake investigations over multiple weeks and could result in a range of products (engineering designs, built objects, spreadsheets,

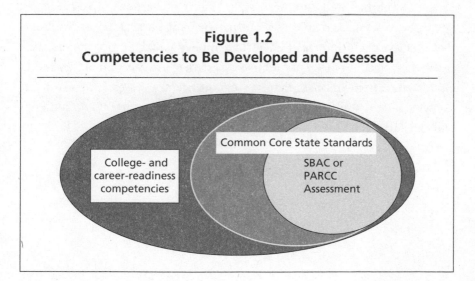

Figure 1.2
Competencies to Be Developed and Assessed

College- and career-readiness competencies

Common Core State Standards

SBAC or PARCC Assessment

research reports) presented in a variety of forms, including oral, graphic, and multimedia presentations.

There are challenges to using performance measures on a much wider scale, such as ensuring the measures' rigor and reliability and managing them in ways that are affordable. At the same time, there are valuable lessons to be learned about how to address such challenges from a growing number of high-achieving nations that have successfully implemented performance assessments, some of them over many decades, as well as from state experiences with performance assessment, programs like the International Baccalaureate and Advanced Placement testing programs, and from the growth of performance measures in the military and other sectors.

These developments have been aided by substantial recent advances in testing technology. This large body of work suggests that performance assessments can pay significant dividends to students, teachers, and policymakers in terms of improvements in teaching, learning, and the quality of information. Research also shows that the assessments can be built to produce confident comparisons of individual student performance over time and comparisons across schools, school systems, and states.

Our goal in this book is to provide an analysis of the prospects and challenges of sustaining performance assessment on a large scale. We describe the history and current uses of performance assessments in the United States and abroad and summarize the results of decades of research on advances in, effects of, and costs of performance assessments. We hope that this work will inform the efforts of policymakers, practitioners, and researchers seeking more productive assessment and accountability models for education—models that can encourage and assess the advanced knowledge and skills that have become critically important for students and can support educators' capacity to develop them.

chapter 2

Defining Performance Assessment

For many people, performance assessment is most easily defined by what it is not: specifically, it is not multiple-choice testing. Rather than choosing among predetermined options, students in a performance assessment must construct an answer, produce a product, or perform an activity.[1] From this perspective, performance assessment encompasses a wide range of activities, from completing a sentence with a few words (short answer), to writing a thorough analysis (essay), to conducting and analyzing a laboratory investigation (hands-on).

Because they allow students to construct or perform an original response rather than just recognizing a potentially right answer out of a list provided, performance assessments can measure students' cognitive thinking and reasoning skills and their ability to apply knowledge to solve realistic, meaningful problems.

Almost every adult in the United States has experienced at least one performance assessment: the driving test that places new drivers into an automobile with a Department of Motor Vehicles official for a spin around the block and a demonstration of a set of driving maneuvers, including, in some parts of the country, the dreaded parallel parking technique. Few of us would be comfortable handing out licenses to people who have passed only the multiple-choice written test also required by states. We understand the value of this performance assessment as a real-world test of whether a person can handle a car on the road. Not only does the test tell us some important things about potential drivers' skills, we also know that preparing for the test helps improve those skills as potential drivers practice to get better. (What parent doesn't remember the hair-raising outings with a sixteen-year-old wanting to practice taking the car out over and over again?) The test sets a standard toward which everyone must work. Without it, we'd have little assurance about what people can actually do with what they know about cars and road rules and little leverage to improve actual driving abilities.

Performance assessments in education are very similar. They allow teachers to gather information about what students can actually do with what they are learning: science experiments that students design, carry out, analyze, and write up; computer programs that students create and test out; research inquiries that they pursue, assembling evidence about a question that they present in written and oral form. Whether the skill or standard being measured is writing, speaking, scientific or mathematical literacy, or knowledge of history and social science research, students perform tasks involving these skills, and the teacher or other rater scores the performance based on a set of predetermined criteria.

A good example of how differently skills are measured on performance assessments as compared to multiple-choice tests is provided by this example from Illinois. The state's eighth-grade science learning standard for technological design reads:

> Technological design: Assess given test results on a prototype; analyze data and rebuild and retest prototype as necessary.

The multiple-choice example on the state test simply asks what "Josh" should do if his first prototype sinks. The desired answer is, "Change the design and retest his boat." The classroom performance assessment, however, says:

> Given some clay, a drinking straw, and paper, design a sailboat that will sail across a small body of water. Students can test and retest their designs.

In the course of this activity, students explore significant physics questions, such as displacement, in order to understand how and why a ball of clay can be made to float. If they are well conducted and carefully evaluated, such activities can combine hands-on inquiry with the demonstration of content knowledge and reasoning skills. They also enable the teacher to assess whether students can frame a problem, develop hypotheses, evaluate outcomes, demonstrate scientific understanding, use scientific facts and terminology, persist in problems solving, organize information, and develop sound concepts regarding the scientific principles in use.

Performance events can take several forms, including requests that can be answered by what are called constructed-response items—those that require students to create a response— within a relatively short time in a traditional on-demand test that students sit down to take. They can also include more extended tasks that require time in class. These performance tasks allow students to engage in more challenging activities that demonstrate a broader array of skills, including problem framing and planning, inquiry, and production of more extended written or oral responses.

WHAT IT MEANS TO TEST HIGHER-ORDER SKILLS

The key issue is not just whether a test expects students to provide an answer to an open-ended prompt or task, but what kind of knowledge and skill the student is expected to exhibit. Educators often refer to lower-level versus higher-order skills. The best-known approach to describing these is Bloom's taxonomy of cognitive skills, shown in figure 2.1.[2] At the bottom of the pyramid, defining lower-level skills, *knowledge* refers to memory and recollection of facts. *Comprehension* refers to demonstrating understanding of these ideas, while *application* refers to using this understanding to complete a task or solve a problem. The depth of understanding increases at each successive level.

The top half of the pyramid represents higher-order skills: *analysis* requires students to examine arguments, make inferences, and find evidence that supports explanations. In the *synthesis* phase, students compile information in different ways to produce a new pattern or alternative solution. *Evaluation* occurs when students weigh and balance evidence, evaluate ideas based on rigorous standards, and present and defend ideas based on their judgments about information.

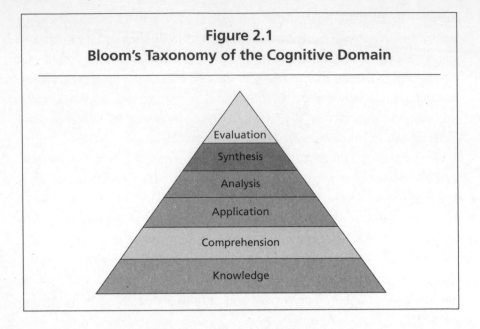

Figure 2.1
Bloom's Taxonomy of the Cognitive Domain

Evaluation

Synthesis

Analysis

Application

Comprehension

Knowledge

One of the differences between many US tests and tests abroad is the extent to which they focus on higher-order skills. For example, a National Science Foundation study found that on an extensive list of standardized mathematics tests, 95 percent of the items tested low-level thinking, 97 percent tested low-level conceptual knowledge, and 87 percent tested low-level procedural knowledge. On science tests, 73 percent of items tested low-level thinking and 77 percent tested low-level conceptual knowledge.[3] These mathematics and science tests almost never assessed the higher-order skills and thinking at the very top of Bloom's taxonomy.

Performance assessments that call for more analysis and manipulation of data and defense of ideas are often advocated because they offer a medium for students to display the higher-order skills of analysis, synthesis, and evaluation.

Even within the genre of performance tasks, cognitive demands can differ. An example can be found in two different constructed response items on physics tests. An item from the New York State Regents Physics exam asks students to draw and label a circuit showing correct locations of resistors, an ammeter, and a voltmeter. Students are then asked to identify the equivalent resistance of the circuit and of a given resistor under specific conditions.[4] This item requires application of knowledge by students; however, it does not go as far in testing higher-order skills as a similar item used on the high school physics examination in Hong Kong, one of the highest-scoring jurisdictions on the Program for International Student Assessment.

First, the Hong Kong item asks students to identify the amount of current flowing through a resistor under different conditions and explain their answers. Next, students are asked to sketch the time variation in the potential difference of the electrical pressure when a switch is opened. Finally, students are asked to show how they would modify the circuit to demonstrate particular outcomes under different conditions.[5] This type of question requires students to demonstrate a greater depth of knowledge, comprehension, application, analysis, and evaluation, using their knowledge flexibly under changing situations, an important twenty-first-century skill.

A CONTINUUM OF ASSESSMENT OPTIONS

Assessment strategies can be thought of as existing along a continuum.[6] At one end are the multiple-choice and close-ended items found in traditional tests. These items measure recall and recognition, but cannot measure higher-level thinking skills or the ability to apply them. At the other end are assessments that require substantial student initiation of designs, ideas, and performances, tapping the planning and work management skills especially needed for college and careers. As shown in figure 2.2, in between, at each step along the continuum, tasks become more complex, measuring progressively larger and more integrated sets of knowledge and skill, more cognitively complex aspects of learning, and more robust applications of knowledge to new problems and situations.

Along this continuum, the role of the student also changes: from passively receiving and responding to external questions, at one end of the continuum, to taking increasing initiative for finding and making sense of information, as well as determining questions, methods, and strategies for investigation, at the other. At the right-hand end of the continuum, where students are conducting substantial research, presenting and defending their work, and revising it in response to feedback, they are also developing

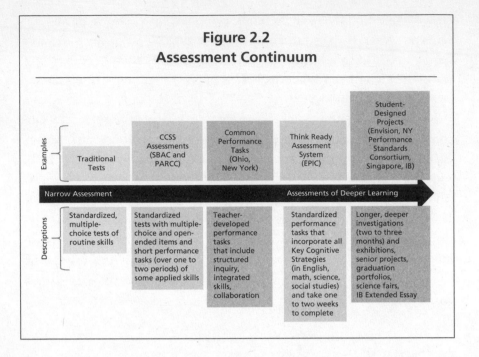

Figure 2.2
Assessment Continuum

| | | | | | Student-Designed Projects (Envision, NY Performance Standards Consortium, Singapore, IB) |
| Examples | Traditional Tests | CCSS Assessments (SBAC and PARCC) | Common Performance Tasks (Ohio, New York) | Think Ready Assessment System (EPIC) | |

Narrow Assessment → Assessments of Deeper Learning

| Descriptions | Standardized, multiple-choice tests of routine skills | Standardized tests with multiple-choice and open-ended items and short performance tasks (over one to two periods) of some applied skills | Teacher-developed performance tasks that include structured inquiry, integrated skills, collaboration | Standardized performance tasks that incorporate all Key Cognitive Strategies (in English, math, science, social studies) and take one to two weeks to complete | Longer, deeper investigations (two to three months) and exhibitions, senior projects, graduation portfolios, science fairs, IB Extended Essay |

and demonstrating a range of communication skills, metacognitive and learning-to-learn skills, resilience that accompanies a growth mind-set with regard to academic pursuits, and in some cases skills of collaboration as well.

These deeper learning skills are demonstrated in the context of robust performance tasks, portfolios, and exhibitions of work that authentically represent how work is developed and evaluated outside of school. Thus, the range of assessment strategies used to evaluate learning and performance must be more extensive than traditional sit-down tests alone can provide.

Rather than trying to have one test address all needs, different methods can be combined in a system of assessments that strategically uses different types of information for different purposes. Performance assessments can be variously designed to provide formative or summative information (or both), gauge student growth on learning progressions, support proficiency determinations, or be combined in a student profile or portfolio.

The types of performance tasks or measures that are useful in a system of assessments can cover a wide span, from a single class period to a semester. They are generally graded by teachers (for their own students or in a system that is moderated across schools for other students) and can yield the kinds of information needed to help inform a range of decisions. Performance tasks may also be subject to some degree of external quality control. This can be accomplished by specifying task content, including creating common tasks at the state or district level; designing the conditions for task administration; managing how tasks are scored; and deciding how results are reported.

The most basic form of performance task may simply require a student to solve a multipart problem and explain his or her solution, write several paragraphs that analyze a piece of text or other evidence, or synthesize and reorganize information into a coherent whole. Even simple tasks assess knowledge and skills that cannot be gauged well with multiple-choice items. Teachers may devise these types of tasks themselves, pull them from curriculum materials, or access them online. They are generally closely tied to the content at hand and require only modest extrapolation and application of terms, ideas, and concepts being learned in class.

Examples of *constructed-response* questions can be found in many large-scale assessments as well. For example, the New York Regents Examinations include constructed-response elements in nearly all subject areas. The US history test, for example, asks students to write essays on topics like the following:

> Discuss the advantages and disadvantages of industrialization
> to American society between 1865 and 1920. In your essay,
> include a discussion of how industrialization affected different
> groups in American society.[7]

Another kind of common constructed-response task occurs in writing tests that require students to formulate and develop ideas and arguments. For example, an English question on the International Baccalaureate exam asks students to choose essay questions within different literary genres and base their answers to questions requiring knowledge of literary techniques on at least two of three works studied in class. Questions like the following are common:

> Using two or three of the works you have studied, discuss how and to what effect writers have used exaggeration as a literary device.

> Acquiring material wealth or rejecting its attractions has often been the base upon which writers have developed interesting plots. Compare the ways the writers of two or three works you have studied have developed such motivations.

> Discuss and compare the role of the speaker or persona in poems you have studied. You must refer closely to the work of two or three poets in your study and base your answer on a total of three or four poems.[8]

Constructed-response items that pose hands-on inquiry tasks can also be used in large-scale settings. On the National Assessment of Educational Progress (NAEP) science test, for example, students are asked to conduct experiments, analyze data, and report results. For example, twelfth-grade students are given a bag containing sand, salt, and three different metals. They are asked to separate the substances using a magnet, sieve, filter paper, funnel, spoon, and water and to document the steps they used to do so. This performance task requires students to conduct experiments using materials provided to them and record their observations and conclusions by responding to both multiple-choice and constructed-response questions. The example demonstrates a hybrid assessment model that tests students' ability to physically conduct an experiment while also testing report writing and factual knowledge that are critical to scientific approaches to problems.

NAEP has also introduced simulations designed to test students' abilities to design experiments, display and interpret results, and search the Internet effectively. One eighth-grade simulation task, for example, required students to investigate why scientists use helium gas balloons to explore outer space and the atmosphere. The following example of an item within this task required students to search a simulated World Wide Web:

> Some scientists study space with large helium gas balloons. These balloons are usually launched from the ground into space but can also be launched from a spacecraft near other planets.
>
> Why do scientists use these gas balloons to explore outer space and the atmosphere instead of using satellites, rockets, or other tools? Be sure to explain at least three advantages of using gas balloons.
>
> Base your answer on more than one web page or site. Be sure to write your answer in your own words.[9]

This task assesses students' online research skills. A related scientific inquiry task required students to evaluate their work, form conclusions, and provide rationales after designing and conducting a scientific investigation:

> How do different amounts of helium affect the altitude of a helium balloon? Support your answer with what you saw when you experimented.[10]

These simulation tasks assess problem-solving, reasoning, and evaluation skills valued within the scientific discipline, providing new possibilities for evaluating student cognition and learning.

Another challenging on-demand assessment of higher-order cognitive skills for both college and high school students has been created by the Council for Aid to Education. The Collegiate Learning Assessment and the College and Work Ready Assessment both use an in-basket approach to evaluate how well students can evaluate a situation, come to a conclusion, and explain their rationale, drawing on multiple sources of evidence of different kinds: textual, graphic, and quantitative. The assessments use two genres of question: Make an Argument (see the example in exhibit 2.1) and Critique an Argument. Both types of tasks allow students to demonstrate their capacity to analyze and synthesize information, weigh and balance evidence, and justify a conclusion or solution.

Exhibit 2.1 Collegiate Learning Assessment Sample Performance Task

You are the assistant to Pat Williams, the president of DynaTech, a company that makes precision electronic instruments and navigational equipment. Sally Evans, a member of DynaTech's sales force, recommended that DynaTech buy a small private plane (a SwiftAir 235) that she and other members of the sales force could use to visit customers. Pat was about to approve the purchase when there was an accident involving a SwiftAir 235. You are provided with the following documentation:

1. Newspaper articles about the accident
2. Federal Accident Report on in-flight breakups in single engine planes
3. Pat's e-mail to you & Sally's e-mail to Pat
4. Charts on SwiftAir's performance characteristics
5. Amateur Pilot article comparing SwiftAir 235 to similar planes
6. Pictures and description of SwiftAir Models 180 and 235

Please prepare a memo that addresses several questions, including what data support or refute the claim that the type of wing on the SwiftAir 235 leads to more in-flight breakups, what other factors might have contributed to the accident and should be taken into account, and your overall recommendation about whether or not DynaTech should purchase the plane.

Source: Collegiate Learning Assessment. (2009). Retrieved from http://www.collegiatelearningassessment .org/.

Moving rightward along the continuum, more ambitious *performance tasks* extending over many days or weeks can test more challenging intellectual skills that come even closer to the expectations for performance found in colleges and careers. For example, the Ohio Performance Assessment Project has developed curriculum-embedded performance tasks at the high school level, aligned to college and workplace readiness standards. In addition to serving as classroom assignments and formative tools, these tasks can serve as components of an end-of-course examination system, an alternative means for students to demonstrate subject matter mastery in a competency-based system, or a way to satisfy the state's senior project requirement.[11]

The Ohio tasks in many ways are similar to those found in European and Asian systems (described in chapter 3). As components of course-based teaching and learning systems, they are designed to measure core concepts and skills in the disciplines that go beyond what can be assessed in a single period on a sit-down test. For example, in English language arts, students apply their understanding of a central theme in American literature to a task that requires selecting, analyzing, interpreting, and explaining texts (see exhibit 2.2).

Exhibit 2.2 Ohio Performance Assessment Project: English Language Arts Performance Task

You are editing an on-line digital anthology for 11–12th graders entitled, "Perspectives on the American Dream." Your job is to prepare the introduction to this anthology. In your introduction, please do the following things:

a. Decide which texts you want to include and in which order (you must include at least *six* texts). Texts can include books, poems, songs, short stories, essays, photographs, articles, films, television shows, or Internet media. The six texts must represent at least two different perspectives and must include at least two different types of text (e.g., print text, visual media, audio media, multi-media, digital media).
b. Identify and discuss different perspectives on the American dream represented in the six texts you selected.
c. Write a short paragraph about each text, in which you make clear why you have included it and how it relates to the other texts in your anthology.
d. Propose a set of questions to focus readers as they consider the perspectives represented in these texts.

Source: Wei, R. C., Schultz, S. E., & Pecheone, R. (2012). *Performance assessments for learning: The next generation of state assessments.* Stanford, CA: Stanford Center for Assessment, Learning, and Equity.

In a mathematics task, students are asked to evaluate how heating costs may change as a simultaneous function of temperature, fuel costs, and savings due to insulation (see exhibit 2.3). The task requires students to apply their knowledge of ratio, proportion, and algebraic functions to a complex, real-world problem. They must engage in analysis and modeling of multiple variables. The response requires a display, explanation, and defense of their ideas.

Exhibit 2.3 Ohio Performance Assessment Project: Heating Degrees Task

Ms. Johnson has installed new insulation to save money on heating costs, but then learns that her bills have not declined by much from the previous year. Her contractor points out that heating costs have risen, and weather has been colder. Ms. Johnson wants to find out how much she has actually saved due to the insulation she installed. Given details about Ms. Johnson's heating bills (rates, units of heat used), temperature changes, and some initial information to research "heating degree days" on the Internet, you have two tasks:

1. Assess the cost-effectiveness of Ms. Johnson's new insulation and window sealing. In your assessment, you must do the following:
    *   Compare Ms. Johnson's gas bills from January 2007 and January 2008.
    *   Explain Ms. Johnson's savings after the insulation and sealing.
    *   Identify circumstances under which Ms. Johnson's January 2008 gas bill would have been at least 10% less than her January 2007 bill.
    *   Decide if the insulation and sealing work on Ms. Johnson's house was cost-effective and provide evidence for this decision.
2. Create a short pamphlet for gas company customers to guide them in making decisions about increasing the energy efficiency of their homes. The pamphlet must do the following:
    *   List the quantities that customers need to consider in assessing the cost-effectiveness of energy efficiency measures.
    *   Generalize the method of comparison used for Ms. Johnson's gas bills with a set of formulas, and provide an explanation of the formulas.
    *   Explain to gas customers how to weigh the cost of energy efficiency measures with savings on their gas bills.

Source: Darling-Hammond, L., Pecheone, R. L., Jacquith, A., Schultz, S., Walker, L., & Wei, R. C. (2010, March). *Developing an internationally comparable balanced assessment system that supports high-quality learning.* Paper presented at the National Conference on Next Generation K–12 Assessment Systems. Washington, DC. Retrieved from http://www.k12center.org/rsc/pdf/Darling-HammondPechoneSystemModel.pdf.

These tasks require students to tackle a substantial, multipart problem and use a range of analytic skills while producing a solution and a product that illustrates and explains their thinking.

Further along the continuum are longer-duration projects that require several weeks or even months of a semester. Often it is the student who defines the focus of the project and is responsible for organizing the task and locating all the necessary information to complete it. The student may be expected to follow a particular outline or address a particular problem or range of requirements in the process of completing the project. The project may be judged by the teacher alone or scored by one or more other teachers in a moderated process that allows teachers to calibrate their scores to a benchmark standard.

For this type of project, a student or team of students might undertake an investigation of locally sourced foods. They would need to research where the food they eat comes from, what proportion of the price represents transportation, how dependent they are on other parts of the country for their food, what choices they could make if they wished to eat more locally produced food, what the economic implications of doing so would be, and whether doing so could cause economic disruption in other parts of the country as an unintended consequence. The project could be presented to the class and scored by the teacher using a guide that included ratings of the use of mathematics and economics content knowledge; the quality of argumentation; the appropriateness of sources of information cited and referenced; the quality and logic of the conclusions reached; and overall precision, accuracy, and attention to detail. A similar interdisciplinary project that addresses a particular problem and its implications is shown in exhibit 2.4.

Exhibit 2.4   Disaster in the Gulf Project

In response to the April 2010 BP Deepwater Horizon oil drilling rig accident, seniors at Envision Schools explored the effects and impact of this event through an interdisciplinary project:

- AP Government: Produce a research paper about our government's role in responding to such a disaster, including the role of federal agencies and our national emergency management system.

(Continued)

- World Literature: Write a three- to four-minute speech using rhetorical skills and deliver the speech at a simulated congressional hearing.
- AP Environmental Science: Explore the environmental impact of the oil spill. Consider different methodologies of cleaning the affected areas, along with the social, economic, and environmental impact of the oil and cleaning.
- Advanced Visual Arts: Create sculptures and other art forms from petroleum-based materials.

This project takes place over nine weeks and is reviewed by the subject-area teacher using a rubric from the College Success Student Performance Assessment System.

_____

Source: Disaster in the Gulf. (2010). Envision Schools.

Finally, a culminating project can be designed to gauge student knowledge and skill cumulatively, including the ability to apply disciplinary standards of practice and modes of inquiry in a subject-specific or interdisciplinary way. Students may study one topic for a semester or even an entire year, applying what they are learning in their academic classes to help them work on the project. The culminating project generally includes a terminal paper and accompanying product and documentation, reflecting overall cognitive development and a range of academic skills.

The results may be presented to a panel that includes teachers, experts from the community, or fellow students. This method of juried exhibitions is used in some examination systems abroad (e.g., in the Project Work task required as part of the International Baccalaureate and the A-level exams in Singapore, described in chapter 3) and by a number of school networks in the United States.[12] Students communicate their ideas in writing, orally, and in other formats (e.g., with the use of multimedia technology or through products they have created), while they demonstrate the depth of their understanding as they respond to questions from others, rather like a dissertation defense.

Such projects may be assembled in a portfolio of work that demonstrates student proficiency across content areas. For example, schools in the New York Performance Standards Consortium require that students complete and defend a graduation portfolio including a literary analysis, a mathematical model, a scientific investigation, and a social science research paper. Some of the consortium schools also require an arts exhibition, a world language demonstration, or a presentation of learning from an internship. Among the assessments, students must provide evidence of competence in oral and written communication, critical thinking, technology use, and other twenty-first-century skills. Across schools, these are evaluated on common scoring rubrics that reflect critical skills in each discipline.

As students repeatedly develop and revise projects and exhibitions evaluated according to rigorous standards, they internalize standards of quality and develop college- and career-ready skills of planning, resourcefulness, perseverance, a capacity to use feedback productively, a wide range of communication skills, and a growth mind-set for learning—all of which extend beyond the individual assignments themselves in shaping their ability to learn in new contexts.

Along a continuum of assessment options, schools, districts, and states can both encourage and evaluate the development of a range of knowledge, skills, and dispositions, collecting evidence for a range of different purposes and supporting instruction focused on twenty-first-century skills.

chapter 3

Experiences with Performance Assessment in the United States and Abroad

There is no shortage of creative ideas for assessing learning and performance in authentic ways. The challenge has been developing and maintaining such assessments at scale in ways that consistently set expectations and provide incentives for deeper learning. If large-scale testing does not incorporate these kinds of performance and if high stakes are attached to large-scale tests, it is very difficult for local schools to preserve and develop instruction focused on higher-order skills.

STATE PERFORMANCE ASSESSMENTS IN THE UNITED STATES

Fortunately, there is much to learn about large-scale performance assessment from state systems in the United States and abroad. As we have noted, a number of states have developed performance assessments as part of their state testing systems, and some of these were preserved in the No Child Left Behind (NCLB) era—for example:

- Maine, Vermont, New Hampshire, and Rhode Island have developed a jointly constructed reference exam, the New England Collaborative

Assessment Program, that includes many constructed-response items. Individual states and districts supplement this exam with state or locally developed performance tasks.

• Rhode Island requires graduation portfolios statewide, developed by each district. New Hampshire has introduced a technology portfolio for graduation that allows students to collect evidence to show how they have met standards in this field, and it is developing a performance assessment system across all content areas. Writing portfolios that assemble student work around specific standards were used for many years in large-scale assessment systems in Vermont and Kentucky.

• Missouri and Kentucky have developed systems of on-demand testing, including substantial constructed-response components, supplemented with state-designed, locally administered performance tasks.

• New York's Regents Exams contain a variety of performance components. The English exam asks students to write three different kinds of essays. The History/Social Studies examinations use document-based questions to elicit essays that reveal students' ability to analyze texts and data, as well as to draw and defend conclusions. Science examinations contain a laboratory performance test.

• Connecticut uses extended writing tasks and rich science tasks as part of its statewide assessment system. For example, during the year, students complete state-developed performance tasks in which they conduct science experiments on specific topics, analyze the data, and report their results to prove their ability to engage in science reasoning. In an end-of-year on-demand test, they carry forward this learning to critique experiments and evaluate the soundness of findings. (See exhibit 3.1.)

Exhibit 3.1   Connecticut Ninth/Tenth Grade Science Assessment: Acid Rain Task

Acid rain is a major environmental issue throughout Connecticut and much of the United States. Acid rain occurs when pollutants, such as sulfur dioxide from coal burning power plants and nitrogen oxides from car exhaust, combine with the moisture in the atmosphere to create sulfuric and nitric acids. Precipitation with a pH of 5.5 or lower is considered acid rain. Acid

---

rain not only affects wildlife in rivers and lakes but also does tremendous damage to buildings and monuments made of stone. Millions of dollars are spent annually on cleaning and renovating these structures because of acid rain.

Your Task

Your town council is commissioning a new statue to be displayed downtown. You and your lab partner will conduct an experiment to investigate the effect of acid rain on various building materials in order to make a recommendation to the town council as to the best material to use for the statue. In your experiment, vinegar will simulate acid rain.

You have been provided with the following materials and equipment. It may not be necessary to use all of the equipment that has been provided.

Suggested Materials	**Proposed Building Materials**
containers with lids	limestone chips
graduated cylinder	marble chips
vinegar (simulates acid rain)	red sandstone chips
pH paper/meter	pea stone
safety goggles	

Designing and Conducting Your Experiment

1. *In your words, state the problem you are going to investigate.* Write a hypothesis using an "If . . . then . . . because . . ." statement that describes what you expect to find and why. Include a clear identification of the independent and dependent variables that will be studied.
2. *Design an experiment to solve the problem.* Your experimental design should match the statement of the problem and should be clearly described so that someone else could easily replicate your experiment. Include a control if appropriate and state which variables need to be held constant.
3. *Review your design with your teacher before you begin your experiment.*
4. *Conduct your experiment.* While conducting your experiment, take notes and organize your data into tables.

(Continued)

(*Continued*)
Communicating Your Findings

Working on your own, summarize your investigation in a laboratory report that includes the following:

1. A statement of the problem you investigated. A hypothesis ("If . . . then . . . because . . ." statement) that described what you expected to find and why. Include a clear identification of the independent and dependent variables.
2. A description of the experiment you carried out. Your description should be clear and complete enough so that someone could easily replicate your experiment.
3. Data from your experiment. Your data should be organized into tables, charts, and/or graphs as appropriate.
4. Your conclusions from the experiment. Your conclusions should be fully supported by your data and address your hypothesis.

Discuss the reliability of your data and any factors that contribute to a lack of validity of your conclusions. Also include ways that your experiment could be improved if you were to do it again.

Students conduct the experiment in a group but write up their results independently, demonstrating their individual understanding. This kind of classroom-embedded task, which all students complete, is scored by teachers using common rubrics. Before NCLB, this assessment was used for state-level and federal reporting. Now the assessments are used for local reporting and may factor into grading rather than for federal accountability purposes. On the end-of-year statewide summative test, students receive a sample of a report from an experiment, which they analyze in terms of the appropriateness of its methods and the validity of its results, drawing on the experiences they have had in the classroom conducting experiments. Thus, the scientific inquiry skills developed through more extensive performance tasks are also evaluated in a less time-intensive way on a more traditional sit-down test.

PERFORMANCE ASSESSMENTS ABROAD

Tasks like this one are similar to the expectations for science inquiry and analysis found in assessment systems in Australia, Canada, England,

Finland, Hong Kong, Singapore, and many other high-performing countries. In fact, the assessment systems of most of the highest-achieving nations in the world are a combination of centralized assessments that use mostly open-ended and essay questions plus local assessments given by teachers, which are factored into the final examination scores. These classroom-based assessments—which include research papers, applied science experiments, presentations, and products that students construct—are mapped to the core curriculum or syllabus and the standards for the subject. They are selected because they represent critical skills, topics, and concepts, and they are evaluated by teachers who are trained and calibrated to score comparably.

External testing is much less frequent in these other nations. It is generally focused on a set of content-based examinations at the end of secondary school, which are sometimes augmented with tests at one or two points in the earlier grades rather than the every-year testing required in the United States. Although the quantity of external testing is much less, the depth and quality are usually much greater. On-demand tests require more elaborate open-ended responses, and classroom tasks often require more student planning and more extensive products.

For instance, Finland's only external test is a voluntary matriculation exam developed jointly by high school and university faculty, which is given at the twelfth-grade level to students who want to go on to college. The open-ended items, which comprise the entire exam, ask students to apply and explain their knowledge in ways that demonstrate a deep understanding of the content under study. As one illustration, mathematics problems require critical thinking and modeling, as well as straightforward problem solving. The basic mathematics exam poses this kind of problem:

> A solution of salt and water contains 25% salt. Diluted solutions are obtained by adding water. How much water must be added to one kilogram of the original solution in order to obtain a 10% solution? Work out a graphic representation which gives the amount of water to be added in order to get a solution with 2–25% of salt. The amount of water (in kilograms) to be added to one kilogram of the original solution

must be on the horizontal axis; the salt content of the new solution as a percentage must be on the vertical axis.[1]

The advanced mathematics exam poses this one:

> In a society the growth of the standard of living is inversely proportional to the standard of living already gained, i.e., the higher the standard of living is, the less willingness there is to raise it further. Form a differential-equation-based model describing the standard of living and solve it. Does the standard of living rise forever? Is the rate of change increasing or decreasing? Does the standard of living approach some constant level?

The classroom-embedded components that supplement on-demand tests in some other countries also demand that students demonstrate their understanding through extensive writing and problem solving. In England, for example, most students aim for the General Certificate of Secondary Education (GCSE), a two-year course of study evaluated by assessments both within and at the end of courses or units. The British system of examinations has informed systems in countries around the world, from Australia, Hong Kong, and Singapore, to the International Baccalaureate and the New York State Regents Examinations.

The GCSE's classroom-based "controlled assessments" emphasize applied knowledge and skills. These are either designed by the awarding body and scored by teachers or designed by teachers and scored by the awarding body, with teachers determining the timing of the assessments. Table 3.1 shows the types of tasks that students complete to fulfill each of the English course units. Together, these comprise 60 percent of the examination score. They result in students' engaging in significant extended writing, as well as speaking and listening, in multiple genres, from texts that are part of the syllabi developed from the national curriculum. Each of these tasks is further specified in terms of what students are asked to do and what criteria are used to evaluate their responses. An external examination body develops and monitors scoring protocols and processes to ensure consistency in evaluation.

Table 3.1 Example of Tasks: GCSE English

Unit and Assessment	Tasks
Reading Literacy Texts	Responses to three texts from set choices of tasks and texts. Candidates must show an understanding of texts in their social, cultural, and historical context.
Imaginative Writing	Two linked continuous writing responses from a choice of text development or media.
Speaking and Listening	Three activities: a drama-focused activity; a group activity; an individual extended contribution. One activity must be a real-life context in and beyond the classroom.
Information and Ideas	Nonfiction and media: Responses to authentic passages. Writing information and ideas: One continuous writing response—choice from 2 options.

Similarly, in Victoria, Australia, on-demand tests are supplemented with classroom-based tasks, given throughout the school year, that comprise at least 50 percent of the examination score. The performance tasks prepare students to succeed on the challenging end-of-course tests that demand high-level applications of knowledge. An example of an item from the high school biology test, for example, describes a particular virus to students; it next asks them to design a drug to kill the virus and explain, in several pages, how the drug operates. Students then design an experiment to test the drug (see exhibit 3.2).

In preparation for this test, students taking biology will have been assessed on six common pieces of work during the school year covering specific outcomes outlined in the syllabus. They will have conducted "practical tasks" like using a microscope to study plant and animal cells by preparing slides of cells, staining them, and comparing them in a variety of ways, resulting in a written product with visual elements. They also will have conducted practical tasks (labs) on enzymes and membranes and on the maintenance of stable internal environments for animals and plants. Finally, they will have completed and presented a research report on characteristics of pathogenic organisms and mechanisms by which organisms can defend against disease. These tasks, evaluated as part of the final examination score, link directly to the expectations that students will encounter on the external examination but go beyond what that examination can measure in terms of how students can apply their knowledge.

Exhibit 3.2 Example from a Victoria, Australia, High School Biology Exam

When scientists design drugs against infectious agents, the term "designed drug" is often used.

A. Explain what is meant by this term: Scientists aim to develop a drug against a particular virus that infects humans. The virus has a protein coat and different parts of the coat play different roles in the infective cycle. Some sites assist in the attachment of the virus to a host cell; others are important in the release from a host cell. The structure is represented in the following diagram:

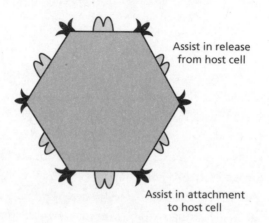

The virus reproduces by attaching itself to the surface of a host cell and injecting its DNA into the host cell. The viral DNA then uses the components of host cell to reproduce its parts and hundreds of new viruses bud off from the host cell. Ultimately the host cell dies.

B. Design a drug that will be effective against this virus. In your answer outline the important aspects you would need to consider. Outline how your drug would prevent continuation of the cycle of reproduction of the virus particle. Use diagrams in your answer. Space for diagrams is provided on the next page.

C. Before a drug is used on humans, it is usually tested on animals. In this case, the virus under investigation also infects mice. Design an experiment, using mice, to test the effectiveness of the drug you have designed.

Source: Darling-Hammond, L., & Wentworth, L. (2010). *Benchmarking learning systems: Student performance assessment in international context.* Stanford, CA: Stanford University, Stanford Center for Opportunity Policy in Education.

Science course examinations in Singapore, as in England and Australia, include an assessment of experimental skills and investigation that counts for 20 to 60 percent of the examination score, depending on the country. Teachers are trained to score these assessments using common criteria under conditions of internal and external moderation for consistency. Following specifications from the Singapore Examinations and Assessments Board, students must:

- Identify a problem, design and plan an investigation, evaluate their methods and techniques.
- Follow instructions and use techniques, apparatus, and materials safely and effectively.
- Make and record observations, measurements, methods, and techniques with precision and accuracy.
- Interpret and evaluate observations and experimental data[2]

Even more ambitious are the Singapore Project Work requirements intended to develop the more advanced thinking skills thought to be underrepresented in the traditional content-based curriculum and examinations system. They represent the goals of reforms launched in 1997 as part of the "thinking schools, learning nation" initiative, which created a number of changes: "Syllabi, examinations and university admission criteria were changed to encourage thinking out of the box and risk-taking. Students are now more engaged in project work and higher order thinking questions to encourage creativity, independent, and inter-dependent learning."[3]

Project Work (PW) is an interdisciplinary subject that is compulsory for all preuniversity students (see exhibit 3.3). Students carry out their collaborative project tasks during dedicated curriculum time. The projects are scored as part of the examination system in high school and can be submitted to the university as part of the application.

Universities are encouraged to examine evidence about student accomplishments beyond examination scores. About twelve thousand students complete this task annually. While the Singapore Examinations and Assessment Board (SEAB) externally specifies task setting, conditions, assessment criteria, achievement standards, and marking processes, classroom teachers carry out the assessment of all three components of PW—the written paper, presentation, and group project file—using a set of assessment criteria provided by the board. All schools are given exemplar material that illustrates the expected marking standards. The board provides training for assessors and internal moderators. Like all other assessments, the grading is both internally and externally moderated.

Exhibit 3.3   Project Work in Singapore

As an interdisciplinary subject, Project Work breaks away from the compartmentalization of knowledge and skills to focus on interdisciplinary outcomes by requiring students to draw on knowledge and apply skills from across different subject domains. The goals for this experience are embedded in the requirements for the task and its assessment, which are centrally set by the SEAB. The tasks are designed to be sufficiently broad to allow students to carry out a project that they are interested in while meeting the task requirements:

- *It must foster collaborative learning through group work.* Together as a group, which is randomly formed by the teacher, students brainstorm and evaluate each other's ideas, agree on the project that the group will undertake, and decide on how the work should be allocated among themselves.
- *Every student must make an oral presentation.* Individually and together as a group, each student makes an oral presentation of his or her group project in the presence of an audience.
- *Both product and process are assessed.* There are three components for assessment:
  - The Written Report, which shows evidence of the group's ability to generate, analyze, and evaluate ideas for the project.
  - The Oral Presentation, in which each individual group member is assessed on his or her fluency and clarity of speech, awareness of audience, as well as response to questions. The group as a whole is also assessed in terms of the effectiveness of the overall presentation.
  - The Group Project File, in which each individual group member submits three documents related to snapshots of the processes involved in carrying out the project. These documents show the individual student's ability to generate, analyze, and evaluate (1) preliminary ideas for a project, (2) a piece of research material gathered for the chosen project, and (3) insights and reflections on the project.

In carrying out the Project Work assessment task, students are intended to acquire self-directed inquiry skills as they propose their own topic, plan their time, allocate individual areas of work, interact with teammates of different abilities and personalities, gather and evaluate primary and secondary research material, and collectively create a product. These processes reflect life skills and competencies, such as knowledge application, collaboration, communication, and independent learning, that prepare students for the future workplace.

The close relationship of these kinds of activities to real-world expectations is what makes them powerful learning experiences that develop transferable skills. As explained by the Hong Kong Educational Assessment Authority, which has recently increased the use of school-based assessments in its examination system:

> The primary rationale for school-based assessments (SBA) is to enhance the validity of the assessment, by including the assessment of outcomes that cannot be readily assessed within the context of a one-off public examination, which may not always provide the most reliable indication of the actual abilities of candidates. . . . SBA typically involves students in activities such as making oral presentations, developing a portfolio of work, undertaking fieldwork, carrying out an investigation, doing practical laboratory work or completing a design project, help students to acquire important skills, knowledge and work habits that cannot readily be assessed or promoted through paper-and-pencil testing. Not only are they outcomes that are essential to learning within the disciplines, they are also outcomes that are valued by tertiary institutions and by employers.[4]

Clearly, performance assessments of these kinds extend beyond traditional notions of testing in the United States.

chapter 4

How Performance Assessment Can Support Student and Teacher Learning

Studies of the implementation of these and earlier performance assessments in California, Connecticut, Kentucky, Maine, Maryland, Missouri, New Hampshire, New York, Ohio, Rhode Island, Vermont, and Washington State have found that both portfolios and performance tasks can be scored reliably by teachers when they are properly designed. (See chapter 5 for a discussion of design and scoring.) Furthermore, as we describe in this chapter, the assessments can support measurable improvements in instruction and student learning by encouraging the teaching of higher-order thinking skills and giving teachers greater insights into how students think, as well as what they understand.[1]

Like the behind-the-wheel test given for all new drivers, performance assessments evaluate what students can do with what they know. The road test not only reveals some important information about drivers' skills; preparation for the test also helps improve those skills as novice drivers practice to get better. In addition, as teachers use and evaluate these tasks, they become more knowledgeable about how to teach to the standards and about their students' learning needs. Thus, the process can improve the quality of teaching and learning.

In the 1990s, when performance assessments were launched in a number of states, studies found that teachers assigned more writing and mathematical problem solving of the kinds demanded on the new assessments in states ranging from California to Kentucky, Maine, Maryland, Vermont, and Washington.[2] Well-designed performance assessments encourage instruction that fosters sophisticated reasoning, problem solving, and communication, as well as activities such as research and writing.[3]

Performance assessments that measure complex thinking skills have been shown to influence student learning as well.[4] School-level studies have found greater increases in performance on both traditional standardized tests and more complex measures for students in classrooms that offer a problem-oriented curriculum that regularly features performance assessment, as compared to other classrooms.[5] On a larger scale, Suzanne Lane and colleagues found that school achievement over a five-year period on the performance-based Maryland State Performance Assessment Program test was strongly related to schools' incorporation of related teaching practices in reading, writing, mathematics, and science.[6] Furthermore, a research team led by testing expert Robert Linn found that these gains carried over to the National Assessment of Educational Progress.[7]

The results of introducing performance assessment have been most positive when states or districts developed teachers' expertise for designing, scoring, and evaluating the results of the assessments.[8] Researchers have found that examining students' work helps teachers learn more about what their students know and can do, as well as how they think. Doing this in the context of standards and well-designed performance tasks stimulates teachers to consider their own curriculum and teaching. Together, teachers can then share specific instructional approaches for supporting the strengths and needs of their students.[9]

HOW ASSESSMENTS CAN STRUCTURE STUDENT LEARNING OPPORTUNITIES

One reason that performance assessments embedded in classroom instruction may help support stronger learning for students is that they ensure that students are undertaking intellectually challenging tasks. If teachers use these kinds of assignments consistently, with feedback and opportunities to revise to meet high standards, the level of rigor in the classroom increases. In addition, these assessments can provide information to teachers regarding how students think and try to solve problems. This feedback allows teachers to diagnose students' strengths as well as gaps in understanding. Because performance assessment tasks often yield multiple ratings in the different domains of performance defined by a rubric, they can also help teachers identify students' strengths and weaknesses. This enables teachers to see more easily what kind of help students need, so they can tailor instruction accordingly.

As we have seen, the growing emphasis on project-based, inquiry-oriented learning in high-performing nations has also caused many of these countries to introduce school-based tasks into their assessment systems: research projects, science investigations, and development of products ranging from software solutions to engineering designs. These tasks, incorporated into examination scores in contexts as far ranging as Britain, Canada, Singapore, Australia, New Zealand, and the International Baccalaureate program, focus teaching and learning on the development of higher-order skills and the use of knowledge to solve problems.

Rather than attempting to keep testing separate from the teaching and learning process, these systems integrate curriculum, instruction, and assessment in ways that improve both teaching and students' learning. The use of curriculum-embedded assessments provides teachers with models of good curriculum and assessment practice, contributes to curriculum equity within and across schools, and allows teachers to see and evaluate student learning in ways that can inform instructional and curriculum decisions. Such curriculum-embedded assessments can also build students' capacity to assess and guide their own learning.

HOW ASSESSMENTS CAN ORGANIZE TEACHER LEARNING

Teachers' engagement in developing, reviewing, scoring, and analyzing the results of students' assessments enables them to understand the standards and develop stronger instruction. Tests are not kept remote and mysterious. Developing, reviewing, and scoring assessments, including those that are used for summative accountability purposes, is part of the work of teaching in these jurisdictions.

Teachers score these open-ended tasks through a process called *moderation*, in which they receive training and then score and discuss model answers until their judgments are reliable—that is, that they accurately represent the standards and are consistent with one another. Sometimes these moderation processes occur within schools; at other times, teachers are assembled from across a region. Teachers use benchmark examples of student work at different levels, along with a rubric or set of scoring criteria, to calibrate their own judgments. As teachers learn to look for the key features of the work expressed in the criteria, they become more aware of the elements of strong student performance. As they continue to score and discuss the work, they fine-tune their capacity to evaluate, so that high rates of reliability are achieved.

Equally important, the scoring process and the discussions around student work help teachers to reflect on their curriculum, teaching, and assessment strategies, thus becoming more effective at teaching the standards.[10] Such involvement heightens the probability that teachers—the critical players for enacting educational change—will come to understand and embrace the standards and be able to use the data from the new assessments. Lauren Resnick, professor and codirector of the Institute for Learning at the University of Pittsburgh, emphasizes this fact in her writings about teachers' work with standards: "Standards documents, even elegant ones with benchmarks and commentary, can affect achievement only if the standards come to be held as personal goals by teachers and students. . . . That will happen only if a concerted effort is made to engage teachers and students in a massive and continuing conversation about what students should learn, what kinds of work they should do, and how well they should be expected to do it."[11]

Involving teachers in scoring assessments is powerful professional development because it connects teachers' learning directly to their examination of student learning and gives them the opportunity to think together about how to improve that learning. It also sends an important message by signaling that teachers can be active participants in shaping change. Acknowledging the critical role of teachers in supporting students' learning, the scoring process puts teachers in their rightful place: at center stage in the school improvement process.

Learning how to use a rubric helps teachers evaluate students' work based on evidence rather than on feelings or assumptions. In the course of scoring, teachers learn to apply common criteria and standards to the work of all their students rather than just comparing students' work to one another. Learning to use evidence as a result of participating in standards-based scoring often transforms the way teachers evaluate student work. As one elementary teacher who participated in a statewide performance assessment of student work project put it, "I moved away from thinking about work in an 'A,' 'B,' 'C,' or 'D' way, to thinking about the criteria for performance and the evidence that would justify my evaluation."[12]

One of the most valuable aspects of this work is the opportunity that scoring sessions provide for collegial conversations. These discussions—which can take place before, during, or after scoring—enable teachers to learn about state or district expectations for their students, hear about how other teachers interpret the standards, and see how the big ideas embodied in standards play out in student work. Working with the standards helps teachers gain a perspective about what is valued and valuable in their broader community. In addition, the scoring experience helps them to develop shared understandings and a common language about the essentials of their disciplines, which develops a sense of professional community and can facilitate more coherent instruction across classrooms.

HOW ASSESSMENTS CAN ILLUMINATE STUDENT THINKING

Scoring worthy tasks gives teachers a window into how their students think as well as what they can do. Well-designed tasks are contextualized in real-world situations, they ask students to show and explain their work, and they offer multiple ways for students to demonstrate their abilities.[13] From this evidence, teachers learn more about the variety of ways students approach and solve problems. Furthermore, because the expectations are publicly articulated, students have a better chance of achieving them. This makes the assessments fairer and more accessible for different kinds of learners.[14]

Many teachers say that participation in scoring motivates them to seek more information about how their students are engaging in learning and how they are thinking. As a New York city middle school teacher remarked after engaging in scoring performance assessments, "I want to make the open-ended questions I ask clear enough to get the information I want to get from the students." And an elementary teacher added, "I will provide more opportunities for revision, self-analysis, and evaluation."

California teachers who participate in the administration and collective scoring of the Mathematics Assessment Resource Service (MARS) performance assessments spend time at the end of the scoring day reflecting on students' successes and challenges and the implications for instruction. Teachers, supervisors, and coaches all see this aspect of the project as valuable for teacher learning. A math coach from an urban school explained:

> We joined the Silicon Valley Mathematics Initiative and decided to give the MARS test. We didn't know what we signed on for or how much work it would be. At one point, I thought we were over our heads. But we continued to forge ahead with the scoring session. I have to say it is one of the most rewarding days I have had in education. [The teachers] really felt they had had an opportunity to explore what was in the students' heads. They came away convinced this way of scoring student work had changed forever the way they will teach.

An assistant superintendent for instruction concurred:

> Scoring the MARS test is the single most valuable professional development we have done with our teachers in mathematics. The full day of scoring the tests led to rich conversations about what we expect from students and how our students think mathematically. We see real buy-in from teachers.

Researchers who have evaluated the MARS process explain how this learning occurs:

> To be able to score a MARS exam task accurately, teachers must fully explore the mathematics of the task. Analyzing different approaches that students might take to the content

within each task helps the scorers assess and improve their own conceptual knowledge. The scoring process sheds light on students' thinking, as well as on common student errors and misconceptions. As one teacher said, "I have learned how to look at student work in a whole different way, to say, 'What do these marks on this page tell me about [the student's] understanding?'" Recognizing misconceptions is crucial if a teacher is to target instruction so that students can clarify their thinking and gain understanding. The emphasis on understanding core ideas helps teachers build a sound sequence of lessons, no matter what curriculum they are using.[15]

Studies have found that as teachers and schools participate in this process, students' mathematics performance improves significantly both on the intellectually challenging MARS tasks and state basic skills tests.[16] As teachers learn how to evaluate student needs and design their instruction to produce stronger mathematical understanding, their students' improvement is stronger. Students of teachers who had received more intensive coaching around formative assessment uses of the tasks had stronger results, as did those who had been taught by teachers with greater involvement in scoring, coaching, and professional development.[17]

In a performance assessment project in Ohio, high school science teachers learn much about their students' learning from participating in scoring sessions of student work on science tasks. As three of them observed:

> I learned how better to apply rubric expectations in my instruction by clarifying what those things "look like" within student examples.

> I learned just how difficult it is for students to do the reflection piece of the project. I will try to construct some models and activities to help students to better accomplish this task.

> Students did a lot of good work, but had trouble labeling and explaining. [I] need to emphasize that more in the classroom.[18]

HOW ASSESSMENTS CAN SUPPORT TEACHING OF DEEPER LEARNING SKILLS

In New England, the Quality Performance Assessment (QPA) initiative has been working with many schools to support changes in curriculum and instruction through the introduction of performance assessments focused on higher-order thinking and performance skills. Many educators who have been engaged with QPA scoring sessions and professional development note that their experience deepened their understanding about how to teach to twenty-first-century skills.

In the Pentucket Regional School District in Massachusetts, for example, six years of engagement with QPA began to change the way in which educators and students approach teaching and learning. Assistant superintendent William Hart notes the power of this work:

> Like a lot of districts, for many years, standardized testing had dominated the thinking of teachers in our district and defined the practices about what kids should know and be able to do. Teachers and administrators had focused their energies on finding the most expedient way to prepare kids for those exams. The unintended impact of this focus was more didactic teaching. As we have engaged in performance assessment development and scoring, a new balance has been brought to people's efforts. Now we assess our students' thinking, collaboration, independence, creative exploration as well as state standards.
>
> Teachers are now using the common rubrics to guide the type of project or task they can develop to marry concept/content acquisition and 21st-century skills. They are asking questions like: "How do I shift the instructional environment to do both? How am I helping kids develop as collaborators?" Measuring worthy skills and knowledge in this way has driven the context of the classroom. The work takes time and collaboration but huge dividends are evident in the student work. And what's interesting is that where performance assessments are being implemented with the greatest fidelity, we are getting the best test performance. . . . The message I take from this is: If you

do performance assessment well, then it is just good teaching and learning, and kids are going to achieve.[19]

In Pentucket, every student in every school has a portfolio of work that demonstrates standards for the district-agreed-upon-habits of learning. This portfolio is presented in a public forum in grades 4, 6, 8, and 11 and is evaluated using rubrics that are common across the district. The public nature of this work also helps parents and family members understand and support their children's learning. Hart explains:

> We have parents attend their children's presentations so that they can see what we do. It is not infrequent that parents leave these events in tears because they are just blown away by the deeper kind of learning and the broader set of skills, attributes, and habits they see that they never before saw in work for the old tests.[20]

As teachers define, teach, and evaluate this broader set of skills, they also learn to measure them based on evidence rather than subjective hunches. As one teacher noted, "[This work] has got me thinking about how to use 21st century skills in my assessments and [how to] grade the work not the kid."[21]

QPA director Laurie Gagnon observed that the conversations that occur around scoring student work strengthen teachers' understanding of these higher level skills:

> There is great power in grounding the conversation in evidence . . . in discussing, "What do I mean by a well-chosen and supported quote? What does it mean to write a good thesis statement? What does this really look like?" Conversations around such questions have yielded big learning for teachers.[22]

HOW ASSESSMENTS CAN CREATE SCHOOL COHERENCE AND A CULTURE OF INQUIRY

Educators also note that using common assessments and rubrics and engaging in collective scoring of student work help to create coherence for the teaching that takes place across grades in a school. Jeanne Sturgess, a staff developer at Souhegan High School in Amherst, New Hampshire, another QPA school, explains:

> Before [working with the QPA initiative] we did not always have consistent alignment of learning outcomes across teams and classes. Teachers might have had rubrics aligned with standards, but the work was not necessarily comparable across classes. The work we have done with QPA over the past two years has focused on trying to ensure that if ninth-grade science teachers are all doing the same project with the same rubrics, they will all make a similar judgment about the students' work. Using common rubrics and performance tasks has created great opportunities for teachers to push their thinking about the level of rigor we ask of students and the level of equity we provide. Although this work presents a huge challenge, the commonness of our work—the shared accountability—offers the best of what standards can bring.[23]

This commonality is supported by the process of moderated scoring of student work. Christina Brown, director of QPA's Principal Residency Network, compares the process of learning to score student work with what happens in umpire school: "[Just as] the prospective umpire learns to distinguish between a ball and a strike, and to know the criteria for what each means, [scorers] learn the details of what proficiency actually looks like."[24]

The effort and time invested in having teachers design common assessment tasks and then score them together using common rubrics yields dividends in regard to both teacher learning and the quality of student outcomes. Amy Woods, an eighth-grade English teacher at Cape Cod Lighthouse Charter School in East Harwich, Massachusetts, speaks to this point:

> We have been doing performance assessment in our school since its inception. At the beginning, each teacher developed his/her own assessments and rubrics and was scaffolding teaching and student assignments differently so that each class was being prepared differently. Now, with our common assessments, we have developed continuity in our rubrics across the

grades. Our collective scoring of that work has given us a common language and more coherence in the school in terms of preparing kids across the continuum of development.[25]

This coherence enables more effective collaboration, which can be a basis for continuous inquiry and improvement. Priti Johari, the redesign administrator for Chelsea High School in Massachusetts, notes that using common performance assessments and rubrics in her school has nurtured not only collaboration but also a culture of inquiry among teachers:

> Our work of creating common assessments and rubrics and scoring them across classrooms has created a culture of inquiry and a collaborative atmosphere. Four years ago classroom doors were closed and there was no collaboration. Twenty-five percent of the teachers in the school were a professional learning community. Now I believe 100 percent of the teachers experience themselves that way. This is a result of our process of learning about the Common Core, unpacking standards, writing lesson plans and tasks, sharing those plans, giving each other feedback, creating common rubrics, and collectively examining student work.[26]

New Hampshire deputy commissioner Paul Leather believes that the performance assessment development and collaborative scoring work currently under way in his state has had a positive impact not only on teacher learning but on student outcomes as well. As evidence for this claim, he points to a decline in New Hampshire's high school dropout rate, an increase in high school graduation rates, and an increase in the number of the state's graduates who go on to college. Leather attributes this to the more personalized teaching that results from the process of teachers' involvement with collaboratively developing and scoring complex performance assessments. He explains:

> [Teachers] are placing a lot more attention on depth of knowledge of the learning process. They are looking at assessment questions: Are we asking students to do things that are going to

be asked of them in the realities of their lives? We are encouraging teachers and students to take on deeper learning. We want to make sure that the assessments we use will incent the kind of teaching we want. This [whole process] has been a breath of fresh air for our teachers as well as our students.[27]

SUMMARY

Teacher involvement in the design, use, and scoring of performance assessments has the potential to address multiple important goals through one concentrated investment: linking instruction, assessment, student learning, and teachers' professional development in high-leverage ways. This approach to performance assessment can support student and teacher learning simultaneously.

By examining the work of their students, teachers increase their knowledge of individual students, become better informed about their students' capacities, and receive guidance about what they need to do next to support students' forward development. Involvement in assessment helps teachers clarify their goals and purposes for teaching, make expectations of students explicit, create learning experiences that apply knowledge to real-life contexts, and provide many different ways for students to demonstrate their abilities and skills. It supports teachers' learning about state standards, their discipline, their students, and their teaching practices. The approach also offers teachers a forum for collaboration and an opportunity to learn. In other words, teacher involvement in standards-based and performance-based assessments lays the groundwork for better teaching and learning. As leaders in the Mathematics Assessment Collaborative note:

> Teachers benefit from this approach as much as students do. . . . Teachers laboring to improve student performance on a high-stakes exam can come to feel isolated, beaten down, and mystified about how to improve. . . . The exigencies of test security mean that teachers often receive little specific information about where their students' performance excelled or fell short. When high-stakes test results come back, often months

after the exam, teachers can do little with the results but regard them as a final grade that marks them as a success or failure.

Assessment that requires students to display their work . . . is a tool for building the capacity of the teaching community to improve its work over time. The discipline of exploring together [what] we want students to know and the evidence of what they have learned is simultaneously humbling and energizing. Knowing that they are always learning and improving creates among educators a healthy, rich environment for change. To improve instruction requires that teachers become wiser about the subject they teach and the ways that students learn it. Performance assessment of students, with detailed formative feedback to teachers accompanied by targeted professional development, helps to build the teacher wisdom we need.[28]

Meeting the Challenges of Performance Assessments

D espite the benefits we have described thus far, legitimate questions and concerns remain about performance assessments. In the late 1980s and early 1990s, many states began to design and implement performance assessments; however, technical concerns, costs, and the demands of testing under No Child Left Behind (NCLB) led many to reduce or abandon performance components of their state accountability systems, even if they were maintained for local use.

Some of the problems that states encountered were due to difficulties with scoring reliability, implementation burdens, and costs; others came from energized stakeholder groups that objected to aspects of the assessments or the manner in which they were implemented. In some states, people objected because the assessments were unfamiliar and stretched the boundaries of traditional testing. In others, the assessments were implemented in ways that did not take account of the needs for educator support, training, and time for participation. Under NCLB, many states had difficulty receiving approval from the federal Department of Education for performance elements of their systems.

But research in the United States and other countries on past and existing performance assessments suggests that these challenges can be overcome and that performance assessments can play an important role in ensuring that the nation's students learn the higher-order skills they need. In this chapter, we describe the advances made and lessons learned.

ACHIEVING RELIABILITY AND VALIDITY

A central concern for any assessment is the credibility of results, which rests in large part on the reliability and validity of the measures—that is, whether they actually measure the skills and knowledge that are intended and whether they do so consistently and comparably across students, schools, tasks, and raters. Researchers agree that well-designed performance assessments offer more valid means to measure many kinds of learning, but many stakeholders have raised concerns about their reliability.

In the early years of performance assessment in the United States, for example, Vermont introduced a portfolio system in writing and mathematics that contained unique choices from each teacher's class. Because of this variation, teachers could not score the portfolios consistently enough to accurately compare schools.[1] Comparable scores were hard to achieve when rating poetry in one class and essays in another.

Since then, studies have reported much higher rates of scoring consistency for more standardized portfolios featuring common task expectations and analytic rubrics, like those that evolved later in Vermont and were ultimately developed in Kentucky. The Kentucky writing portfolio is a set of common performance tasks: three writing samples in different genres, with specific guidelines for each task and specific rubrics for scoring them. Over time, with teacher training and a statewide audit system, reliability increased to the point that auditors who randomly rescored selected portfolios showed rates of agreement with the original ratings of 99 percent for exact or adjacent scores.[2]

When performance assessments are used to judge schools and students, testing officials must develop strategies for standardizing the content that is measured, the administration of the assessments, and the scoring of student performances over time to ensure the quality and validity of the scores. This is not easy to do on a large scale with tests that require students to construct their own answers, because such tests often require human scorers. But improvements in test administration and scoring are improving the viability of large-scale performance assessments.

Researchers working in this field have found methods that help ensure the quality of performance tasks, producing more valid and stable results for a wide range of students.[3] In this section, we describe advances that have been made in these areas over the past two decades of work on performance assessments.

Task Design

A high-quality performance assessment is based on what we know about student learning and cognition in the specific domain, as well as a clear understanding of the specific knowledge and skills (or construct) to be assessed, the purpose of the assessment, and the interpretations to be drawn from the results. It is closely aligned to the relevant curriculum.[4] It also is built to reduce what is known as "construct irrelevant variance"— that is, aspects of a task that might confuse the measurement of the central knowledge or skill being assessed. For example, the use of unnecessarily complicated vocabulary or syntax in a task may undermine the accurate measurement of mathematics skills for English learners. Simplifying the language while retaining the central features of the mathematics to be evaluated makes the task a more valid measure.

Assessments are stronger when test specifications are clear about what cognitive skills, subject matter content, and concepts are to be assessed and what criteria define a competent performance.[5] Specifications of content, skills, and criteria can guide templates and scoring rubrics that are used with groups of tasks that measure the same sets of skills. Rubrics and templates help ensure that the content of the assessment is comparable across years to allow for measuring change in student performance over time.[6]

Suzanne Lane gives an example of a template for an "explanation task."[7] It asks students to read one or more texts that require some prior knowledge of the subject domain, including concepts, principles, and declarative knowledge, in order to understand them, and to evaluate and explain important issues introduced in the text. Consider an explanation task developed in Hawaii:[8]

> Imagine you are in a class that has been studying Hawaiian history. One of your friends, who is a new student in the class, has missed all the classes. Recently, your class began studying

the Bayonet Constitution. Your friend is very interested in this topic and asks you to write an essay to explain everything that you have learned about it.

Write an essay explaining the most important ideas you want your friend to understand. Include what you have already learned in class about Hawaiian history and what you have learned from the texts you have just read. While you write, think about what Thurston and Liliuokalani said about the Bayonet Constitution, and what is shown in the other materials.

Your essay should be based on two major sources:

1. The general concepts and specific facts you know about Hawaiian history, and especially what you know about the period of Bayonet Constitution.

2. What you have learned from the readings yesterday.

Prior to receiving this task, students were required to read the primary source documents referred to in the prompt. This task requires students not only to make sense of the material from multiple sources but to integrate material from these multiple sources in their explanations. This provides just one example of a task that can be generated from the explanation task template. An assessment system could use this type of task each year and replace the content while maintaining the central features of the task.

Task Review and Field Testing

Researchers have found that more valid and reliably scored tasks result from careful review and field testing of items and rubrics to ensure that they measure the knowledge and skills intended. This includes interviewing students as they reflect on what they think the task is asking for and how they tried to solve it.[9] The individual piloting of tasks also provides an opportunity for the examiner to pose questions to students regarding their understanding of task wording and directions and to evaluate their appropriateness for different subgroups of students, such as students whose first language is not English.

Large-scale field testing provides additional information regarding the quality of the tasks, including the psychometric characteristics of items.

This includes analyzing student work to ensure that the tasks evoke the knowledge and skills intended and that the directions and wording are clear, and testing different versions of tasks to see which work best across different groups of learners. When these processes are followed, developers have been able to create tasks that are more clearly valid for their intended purposes and are more reliably scored.

Scoring

Perhaps the most frequently asked question surrounding these assessments is how to ensure comparability in scoring across different raters. Most of the systems described earlier, in both the United States and abroad, use common scoring guides, or rubrics, and engage graders in training, calibration, and moderation processes to ensure consistency.

Much has been learned about how to establish effective processes of training and moderation. We noted earlier the strong interrater reliability was achieved in the Kentucky writing portfolio, for example, which consists of a set of tasks within specified genres, with well-constructed scoring rubrics, teacher-moderated scoring processes, and a strong audit system that provides feedback to schools. Many developers of performance assessments have learned how to manage these processes in ways that achieve interrater reliabilities at or above 90 percent, matching the level achieved in the Advanced Placement system and on other long-standing tests.[10]

Human scoring of performance tasks has been found to be highly reliable when tasks are standardized and scorers are effectively trained to share a common understanding of the scoring rubric so as to apply it consistently. Valid and reliable scoring is also enhanced by the design of quality scoring rubrics. Such rubrics:

- Are designed for a family of tasks or a particular task template.
- Include criteria aligned to the processes and skills that are to be measured—for example, in a mathematics task, students' computational fluency, strategic knowledge, and mathematical communication skills.
- Develop criteria for judging the quality of the performance with the involvement of content and teaching experts who

know the domain and understand how students of differing levels of proficiency would approach the task.

- Identify score levels that reflect learning progressions as well as each of the important scoring criteria.
- Are validated through research with a range of students.[11]

A variety of systems for calibration and moderation of teacher scoring exist around the world. In New York State, teacher scoring of Regents Examinations has been conducted at the school or regional level following training and is supplemented by a regular audit of scores from the state department of education, which can follow up with both rescoring and retraining of teachers. In Alberta, Canada, teachers have convened in centralized scoring sessions that involve training against benchmark papers and repeated calibration of scores until high levels of consistency are achieved. All scoring occurs in these sessions, with "table leaders" continually checking and rechecking the scoring for consistency while it is going on.

In England and Singapore, similar strategies are used, with benchmark papers and student "record files," including student work that has already been evaluated in relation to score points on learning progressions. These materials are used to train teachers to recognize the meaning of each score point and to calibrate scoring. In addition, moderation processes are used within schools for teachers to calibrate their scores to benchmarks and to each other, while external moderators also examine schools' scored examinations and initiate additional training where it is needed. At the high school level, examination boards perform these functions of training and calibrating scorers.

In Queensland, Australia, samples of performance tasks from schools are rescored by panels of expert teachers who guide feedback to schools and potential adjustments in scores. In Victoria, Australia, the quality and appropriateness of the tasks, student work, and grades is audited through an inspection system, and schools are given feedback on all of these elements. In both of these jurisdictions, statistical moderation is used to ensure that the same assessment standards are applied to students across schools. The schools' results on external exams are used as the basis for this moderation, which adjusts the level and spread of each school's performance assessments of its students to match the level and spread of the same students' collective scores on the common external test score.

In the International Baccalaureate program, which operates in 125 countries, teachers receive papers to score through computer delivery, and they calibrate their scoring to common benchmarks through an online training process that evaluates their ability to score accurately. The teachers upload their scored papers to be further evaluated or audited as needed and to have the scores recorded. Similarly, in Hong Kong, most delivery and scoring of open-ended assessments is becoming computer based, as it is in twenty other provinces of China. There, as in many other places, double scoring is used to ensure reliability, with a third scorer called in if there are discrepancies.

More recently, automated scoring procedures have been developed to score both short and long constructed-response items. Automated scoring has been used successfully in contexts ranging from state end-of-courses exams to the Collegiate Learning Assessment (CLA)[12] and the National Assessment of Educational Progress (NAEP)—in both the Math Online project that required students to provide explanations of their mathematical reasoning and the NAEP simulation study that required students to use search queries.[13] In the NAEP study that used physics simulations, the agreement between human raters and computer ratings in a cross-validation study was 96 percent. In the more complex extended CLA task, correlations of human and computer ratings were also high, at 86 percent.[14]

Measuring Growth

There is much work to be done on assessments generally to ensure that they can better measure gains in student learning. The problem with many tests currently used to measure gains is that they may measure items that reflect what states define as grade-level standards, but they do not measure student progress along a well-justified scale representing growing understanding of concepts or development of skills. These concerns are true regardless of the kinds of item types being used.

Some assessment experts, like Robert Mislevy, argue that performance assessments can provide better measurement of growth and change in higher-order cognitive abilities and problem-solving strategies based in part on analyses of the numbers and kinds of strategies students use.[15] Others have pointed out the potential for advances in measuring growth by designing performance assessments that reflect learning progressions. Learning progressions indicate what it means to acquire understanding within a content domain, and they identify where a student is on the continuum of the underlying construct. The progress map shown in exhibit 5.1 illustrates a learning progression from Australia's Developmental Assessment program. A student's progress in understanding number concepts can be charted on this continuum, which provides a picture of individual growth against a backdrop of normatively established expectations.[16]

These kinds of progressions can be used, as they have been in Australia and England, to design content standards and performance tasks that measure gains in students' learning as they develop understanding and competency in the content domain.[17] Furthermore, they have the potential to lead to more meaningful scaling of assessments that span grade levels, and thus more valid score interpretations regarding student growth. Research and development that builds on the work already under way in other countries could allow significant progress on this front.

Exhibit 5.1   Progress Map for Counting and Ordering

The lower portion of a counting and ordering progress map follows. It shows examples of knowledge, skills, and understandings in the sequence in which they are generally expected to develop from grades 1 through 5. This type of map is useful for tracking the progress of an individual child over time. An evaluation using tasks designed to tap specific performances on the map can provide a snapshot showing where a student is located on the map, and a series of such evaluations is useful for assessing a student's progress over the course of several years.

1. Counts collections of objects to answer the question "How many are there?"
    Makes or draws collections of a given size (responds correctly to "Give me 6 bears")
    Makes sensible estimates of the size of small collections up to 10 (for 7 buttons, 2 or 15 would not be a sensible estimate, but 5 would be)
    Skip counts in 2s or 3s using a number line, hundred chart, or mental counting (2, 4, 6, . . .)
    Uses numbers to decide which is bigger, smaller, same size (If he has 7 mice at home and I have 5, then he has more)
    Uses the terms *first, second, third* (I finished my lunch second)

---

2. Counts forward and backward from any whole number, including skip counting in 2s, 3s, and 10s

   Uses place value to distinguish and order whole numbers (writes four ten dollar notes and three one dollar coins as $43)

   Estimates the size of a collection (up to about 20)

   Uses fractional language (one-half, third, quarter, fifth, tenth) appropriately in describing and comparing things

   Shows and compares unit fractions (finds a third of a cup of sugar)

   Describes and records simple fractional equivalents (The left-over half pizza was as much as two quarters put together)

3. Counts in common fractional amounts (two and one-third, two and two-thirds, three, three and one-third)

   Uses decimal notation to two places (uses 1.25 m for 1 m 25 cm; $3.05 for three $1 coins and one 5 cent coin; 1.75 kg for 1750 kg)

   Regroups money to fewest possible notes and coins (11 × $5 +17 × $2 + 8 × $1 regrouped as 1 × $50 + 2 × $20 + $5 + $2)

   Uses materials and diagrams to represent fractional amounts (folds tape into five equal parts, shades 3 parts to show 3/5)

   Expresses generalizations about fractional numbers symbolically (1 quarter = 2 eighths and 1/4 = 2/8)

4. Counts in decimal fraction amounts (0.3, 0.6, 0.9, 1.2, . . .)

   Compares and orders decimal fractions (orders given weight data for babies to two decimal places)

   Uses place value to explain the order of decimal fractions (Which library book comes first—65.6 or 65.126? why?)

   Reads scales calibrated in multiples of ten (reads 3.97 on a tape measure marked in hundredths, labeled in tenths)

   Uses the symbols =, <, and > to order numbers and make comparisons (6.75 < 6.9; 5 × $6 > 5 × $5.95)

   Compares and orders fractions (one-quarter is less than three-eighths)

5. Uses unitary ratios of the form 1 part to X parts (the ratio of cordial to water was 1 to 4)

   Understands that common fractions are used to describe ratios of parts to whole (2 in 5 students ride to school. In school of 550, 220 ride bikes.)

   Uses percentages to make straightforward comparisons (26 balls from 50 tries is 52%; 24 from 40 tries is 60%, so that is better)

   Uses common equivalences between decimals, fractions, and percentages (one-third off is better than 30% discount)

   Uses whole number powers and square roots in describing things (finds length of side of square of area 225 sq cm as a square root of 225)

Source: Adapted from *Mathematics - a curriculum profile for Australian schools,* Curriculum Corporation, Victoria 1994, pp 26, 40, 56, 70, 86. Reproduced with permission from Education Services Australia, 2014.

Consequences of Assessment

Fundamental to the validation of test use is the evaluation of the intended and unintended consequences of the use of an assessment, known as "consequential validity."[18] Because performance assessments are intended to improve teaching and student learning, it is important to obtain evidence of whether they have these positive effects or any negative effects.[19]

Research from the New York Performance Standards Consortium indicates that New York City students who graduate from these schools (which have a much higher graduation rate than the city as a whole, although they serve more low-income students, students of color, and recent immigrants) are more successful in college than most students nationally.[20] Students point to the research papers and exhibitions they have had to complete, along with the feedback and revision process, leading to and sometimes following the defense, as key elements in their success.

As these students and others indicate, the clear criteria and rubrics that accompany good performance tasks can help students improve their work, especially if these carry over across multiple formative and summative assessments over time. For example, if writing is repeatedly evaluated for its use of evidence, accuracy of information, evaluation of competing viewpoints, development of a clear argument, and attention to conventions of writing, students begin to internalize the criteria and guide their own learning more productively. As an example of how this process can operate, one study found that the introduction of such evaluation criteria produced significantly larger gains in individual learning scores as students spent more time discussing content, discussing the assignment, and evaluating their products.[21]

An analysis of dozens of studies by British researchers Paul Black and Dylan Wiliam found that the regular use of these kinds of open-ended assessments with clear criteria to guide feedback, student revision, and teachers' instructional decisions, called formative assessments, produces larger learning gains than most instructional interventions that have been implemented and studied.[22]

For perhaps similar reasons, studies have found that teachers who were involved in scoring performance assessments with other colleagues were enabled to understand standards and the dimensions of high-quality work more fully and to focus their teaching accordingly.[23]

These potentially positive consequences of performance assessments signal possibilities, however, not certainties. The quality of the assessments, how well they are constructed, and how thoughtfully they are implemented all influence the outcomes of assessment use and must be taken into account.

ENSURING FAIRNESS

To make assessments fair and valid, it is important to eliminate features that can affect performance but are not related to the specific knowledge and skills being measured. Problems can arise due to task wording and context, the mode of response required, and raters' attention to irrelevant features of responses or performances. As an example, in designing a performance assessment that measures students' mathematical problem solving, tasks should be set in contexts that are familiar to the population of students. If one or more subgroups of students are unfamiliar with a particular problem context, it can affect their performance and hinder the validity and fairness of the score interpretations for those students. Similarly, if a mathematics performance assessment requires a high level of reading ability and students who have very similar mathematical proficiency perform differently due to differences in their reading ability, the assessment is measuring in part a construct that is not the target, namely, reading proficiency.

These issues are of particular concern for English Language Learners (ELLs). Although there are legitimate concerns about the linguistic demands of performance assessments, some studies have found that this is no more a problem with open-ended prompts than with traditional tests. For example, one recent study found that student responses to a writing prompt were less affected by student background variables, including English learner status, than were scores on a commercially developed language arts test, largely consisting of multiple-choice items.[24]

In fact, as testing expert Jamal Abedi explains, several components of well-designed performance assessments can make them more accessible to ELL students than multiple-choice assessments.[25] First, in many performance assessments, language is not the only medium of assessment. As noted, many tasks incorporate graphical or hands-on elements as a different medium through which an ELL student can engage the content being tested and respond to the tasks. Drawing graphical representations of relationships as in some of the mathematics items shown earlier, or physically completing a science activity, such as sorting and categorizing substances, as in the NAEP science task described above, allows students to demonstrate knowledge in multiple ways.

Second, multiple-choice tests often include responses that are plausibly correct, where the respondent is supposed to choose the best of several reasonable responses, or distractor choices that are intended to fool a respondent who is not reading carefully. These can often be particularly problematic for new English learners or students with disabilities who may know the material but cannot draw the fine linguistic distinctions that are required.

Finally, on performance assessments, raters can evaluate what respondents show about what they know, which allows them to credit students with the knowledge they can illustrate (e.g., a solution on a mathematics problem) rather than getting only a count of right and wrong answers without information about the students' actual ability to read a passage or solve a problem. Particularly for special populations of students, scores on proxy items that are further from a direct performance can be deceiving because they do not reveal whether the student understood all or part of the material but was confused by the instructions, format, or wording of the question or response choices, or may have made a minor error in the course of responding.

For these reasons, ELL students and students with disabilities sometimes perform better on performance tasks. This has proved the case in the New Jersey Special Review Assessments offered to students who fail the state high school exit exam. These open-ended performance tasks test the same standards and concepts as items on the multiple-choice test, but have proved more accessible to these populations of students. (See exhibit 5.2 for a task example.)

In any kind of test, careful design can make a difference in validity for special populations. Jamal Abedi and his colleagues have identified a number of linguistic features of test items that slow readers down and increase the chances of misinterpretation. They have found that linguistic modifications that reduce the complexity of sentence structures and replace unfamiliar vocabulary with more familiar words increase the performance of English learners, as well as other students in low- and average-level classes.[26] Linguistic modifications can be used in the design of performance assessments to help ensure a valid and fair assessment, not only for ELLs but other students who may have difficulty with reading.

Exhibit 5.2 shows how a task from the New Jersey SRA can be made even more accessible with linguistic modifications without altering the knowledge and skills being measured. These modifications reduce the length of the task instructions by more than 25 percent, eliminate conditional clauses and grammatical complexities (such as passive voice), and use more familiar words. The modified task that is easier to read nevertheless tests the same mathematics skills.

Exhibit 5.2 New Jersey Department of Education, 2002–2003 SRA Mathematics Performance Assessment Task

Original Item

Dorothy is running for president of the student body and wants to create campaign posters to hang throughout the school. She has determined that there are four main hallways that need six posters each. A single poster takes one person 30 minutes to create and costs a total of $1.50.

A. What would be the total cost for Dorothy to create all the needed posters? Show your work.

B. If two people working together can create a poster in 20 minutes, how much total time would Dorothy save by getting a friend to help her? Show your work.

C. If Dorothy works alone for 3 hours, and is then joined by her friend, calculate exactly how much total time it will take to create all the necessary posters. Show your work.

D. Omar, Dorothy's opponent, decided to create his posters on a Saturday and get his friends Janice and Beth to help. He knows that he can create 24 posters in 12 hours if he works alone. He also knows that Janice can create 24 posters in 10 hours and Beth can create 24 posters in 9 hours. How long will it take them, if all three of them work together to create the 24 posters? Round all decimals to the nearest hundredths. Show your work.

E. When Omar went to purchase his posters, he discovered that the cost of creating a poster had increased by 20%. How many posters will he be able to create if he wants to spend the same amount of money on his posters as Dorothy? Justify your answer.

(Continued)

Linguistically Modified Item

You want to plant 6 roses in each of four large pots. Planting a single rose takes you 30 minutes and costs $1.50.

A. What is the total cost to plant all roses? Show your work.
B. With a friend's help, you can plant a rose in 20 minutes. How much total time do you save by getting a friend to help? Show your work.
C. You work alone for 3 hours, and then a friend joins you. Now how much total time will it take to plant all the roses? Show your work.
D. You can plant 24 roses in 12 hours. Your friend Al can plant 24 in 10 hours and your friend Kim can plant 24 roses in 9 hours. How long does it take the three of you to plant 24 roses together? Round all decimals to the nearest hundredths. Show your work.
E. You just discovered that the cost of purchasing a rose increased by 20%. How many roses can you plant with the same amount of money that you spent when a rose cost $1.50? Justify your answer.

Source: Abedi, J. (2010). *Performance assessments for English language learners.* Stanford: Stanford University, Stanford Center for Opportunity Policy in Education.

Finally, as Abedi points out, performance assessments provide stronger information for diagnostic purposes to help teachers decide how to continue instruction. They reveal more about students' processing skills and problem-solving approaches, as well as their competence in particular areas, than do multiple-choice responses. They also simulate learning activities, and as part of a system, they may encourage teachers to use more complex assignments or formative assessments that resemble the tasks. These characteristics of performance assessments can be particularly beneficial for special needs student populations, including ELLs, because they provide more equitable learning opportunities and give teachers more information about how to support further learning.[27]

In general, fairness concerns can be addressed both by ensuring that all students gain access to rich assignments and learning opportunities—a goal supported by the use of classroom-based performance assessments—and by expert design of the tasks and rubrics and analyses of student thinking as they solve performance tasks. Use of universal design features, such as linguistic modifications, and pilot testing that leads to modifications of tasks based on features that contribute to subgroup differences also increases fairness.

SUPPORTING FEASIBILITY

A host of feasibility issues have cropped up with performance assessment efforts in the United States, including the reliable production of high-quality tasks that are generalizable and scorable, managing the time and costs of scoring open-ended items, and ensuring that assessments can be well implemented by teachers without overwhelming them. Feasible systems also need to take advantage of efficiencies that have been discovered in assessment development, administration, and scoring, discussed here and further in chapter 6.

Efficiencies in Task Design

A number of advances can make performance assessments more efficient and effective as both measurement and teaching tools. For example, tasks can be designed to yield scores on different dimensions of performance in more than one content domain, which has practical as well as pedagogical appeal. Well-designed tasks that yield multiple scores reduce the time and costs of task development, test administration, and scoring by raters.[28] Tasks that cut across content domains may also motivate a more integrated approach to teaching and learning.

For example, a text-based writing task in the Delaware state assessment was linked to a passage in the reading assessment, and student responses to the task were scored twice, once for reading and once for writing. This task, shown below, required students to read an article prior to writing:

> The article you have just read describes some problems and possible solutions for dealing with grease. Do you think grease should be classified or labeled as a pollutant?
>
> Write a letter to the Environmental Protection Agency explaining whether or not grease should be classified as a pollutant. Use information from this article to support your position.[29]

This task is aligned to the reading and writing connection that occurs in instruction in Delaware classrooms. Students are first asked to read about a topic and then to use the information that they have read to support their position in their written product.

ETS researchers are currently developing methods that allow for accurate student level scores derived from mathematics and language arts performance assessments that are administered on different occasions throughout the year.[30] This will not only allow more content representation across the performance assessments, but the assessments can be administered in closer proximity to the relevant instruction, and information from any one administration can be used to inform future instructional efforts. In the future, assessments may provide both formative benefits and summative scores in a more integrated and efficient way that supports teachers.

Technological Advances

Advances in computer technology have made possible other efficiencies in measurement of performance. These advances have permitted performance-based simulations that assess problem-solving and reasoning skills in both formative assessments and summative assessment programs. The most prominent large-scale assessments using computer-based simulations occur in licensure examinations in medicine, architecture, and accounting. In medicine, for example, the prospective doctor is presented with a description of the patient and then must manage the patient's case by selecting history and physical examination options or by making entries into the patient's chart to request tests, treatments, and consultations as needed. The condition of the patient changes in real time based on the patient's disease and the examinee's actions. The computer-based system generates a report that displays each action the examinee takes and scores the appropriateness of the decisions made.

In addition to evaluating a student's responses, new technologies allow assessments to capture students' processes and strategies, along with their products. The computer can monitor and record the interactions a student has with tools used in solving a problem, assessing how students use these tools.[31] Teachers can use information on how a student arrived at an answer to guide instruction and monitor the progression of student learning.[32]

Computer technologies can also be used to create effective and efficient systems of online training, calibration, and scoring for performance items that save time and money. It is now possible to have tasks uploaded by students and sent to teachers who will download and score them—often at home over a cup of coffee. These same teachers will have learned to score through online training and the computer will have certified their grading as reliable. The scored tasks they upload can be audited at any time to ensure that assessments are being scored consistently.

Finally, the use of automated scoring procedures for evaluating student performances in computer-based simulation tasks can provide an answer to the cost and time demands of human scoring. To ensure fairness in the brave new world of computer adaptive testing, it is important that examinees have had the opportunity to practice with the navigation system.[33] Advances in artificial intelligence can help reduce scoring burdens and enable faster turnaround even though the requirements of complex programming do not yet produce much reduction in costs (see chapter 6).

At the same time, using teachers as scorers can reduce costs (see chapter 6) while it helps improve instruction and communication. Teachers who are trained to score assessments internalize the meaning of standards as they gain a better understanding of student thinking and misconceptions that can guide instruction. The rubrics used in scoring performance tasks support collaboration and learning among teachers by providing a unified language and common framework for them to recognize, debate, and assess student work.[34]

Teachers do not have to score 150 of the same items to gain these benefits. They might be asked to score a subsample of the tasks that are otherwise scored by computer, as both ongoing checks on the validity of computer scoring and a learning opportunity for themselves. In the future, it will be possible to organize assessments that use a strategic blend of machine and human scoring that supports opportunities for teacher engagement while reducing burdens.

Creating State Capacity

Experiences with performance assessments from New York, Kentucky, Massachusetts, Vermont, and other states provide a wealth of lessons about how to develop and administer assessments, involve teachers in professional development, and create systems that can support ongoing testing practices.

New York is an interesting case given its 135-year history of assessments that include performance elements. Early in its history, all of New York's tests were open-ended essay examinations and problem solutions developed and scored by teachers under state coordination. Today the syllabus-based, end-of-course Regents Exams in English, Global History and Geography, US History and Government, Mathematics, and Science may be the closest US equivalent to the British system. All New York teachers participate in all aspects of the Regents testing process, from item and task development to review and training, as well as scoring. Teachers score on professional development days when they are released from teaching, and there are auditing systems that sample papers for rescoring that may be followed by score adjustments and further training. A similar process in Kentucky, with substantial teacher training using benchmark performances and common scoring guides, as well as ongoing auditing, has resulted in high levels of consistency in scoring, as well as more common understandings about high-quality work among teachers.

Systems that create consistent local scoring across schools, and hence comparability of results, require substantial planning. States must commit to teacher training and, ideally, to moderation sessions that bring teachers together to score so that they can learn with one another. After training, states may decide to use only those certified scorers who demonstrate they can score reliably to common benchmarks. States must also provide a systematic approach to auditing scores, providing feedback, and adjustments needed to yield consistent scoring across a state. There is evidence that well-designed, consistent processes yield increasingly comparable scoring over time as the standards and processes are internalized by teachers and incorporated into instruction. The phasing in of performance assessment components of larger assessment systems should allow time for a state not only to refine and improve audit procedures, but also for local educators to internalize the state's general standards of performance.

chapter 6

Making High-Quality Assessment Affordable

Many policymakers have argued that the extensive use of performance items is too expensive in large-scale testing. However, expenditures on testing are a tiny fraction of spending on education. With spending on education averaging just over $10,000 per pupil, $25 in combined testing costs for math and reading, the average for most states under No Child Left Behind (NCLB), represents less than one-quarter of 1 percent of the K–12 education—less than the cost of half a tank of gas for the family car. To get a sense of the relative size of this investment, think about the fact that most of us spend at least $300 a year for routine checkups on our automobiles— more than ten times what we spend to find out what students have learned in our state education systems.

Ironically, the tiny investment in state testing has an enormous influence on instruction given the accountability policies that attach important consequences to scores. Multiple-choice tests, while inexpensive, produce few incentives to encourage instruction focused on higher-order thinking and performance skills. Open-ended assessments—essay exams and performance tasks—are more expensive to score, but they can support more ambitious teaching and learning. As a benchmark for the market price of more open-ended measures aimed at higher-order learning, Advanced Placement exams, which typically include essay components and may include a portfolio of work, are priced at about $90 per assessment; student participation in each of the International Baccalaureate assessments, which including open-ended responses and project-based components, costs about $100.[1]

Yet large investments are not essential for states to offer much higher-quality assessments. Studies show that states and districts together are now spending as much as or more on low-quality tests as they would need to spend on much higher-quality assessments if they organized their efforts more thoughtfully and efficiently. Recent estimates from two separate studies put average state spending on English language arts (ELA) and math tests at $25 to $27 per pupil, with a range across states from about $13 to $105 per pupil.[2] In addition, state and local spending on interim and benchmark tests adds an additional $17 to $18 per pupil, not counting the costs of test preparation materials, personnel for test administration and analysis, or teacher time for scoring or professional development associated with this testing.[3] When these expenditures are included, the combined costs of state and local testing in ELA and mathematics alone exceed $50 per pupil on average. (See figure 6.1.)

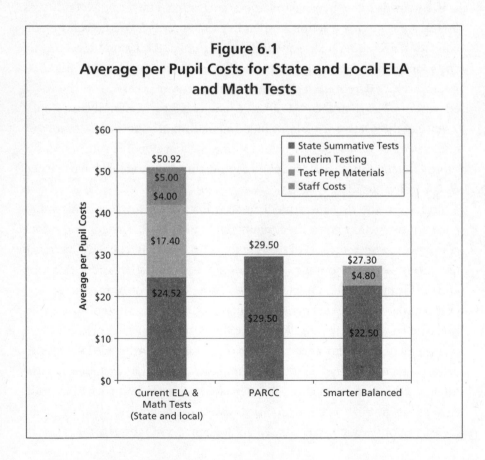

Figure 6.1
Average per Pupil Costs for State and Local ELA
and Math Tests

As we detail, this level of spending could support higher-quality assessments that include the kinds of open-ended items and performance tasks that can measure more complex learning, scored by both teachers and by the evolution of more sophisticated artificial intelligence (AI) engines. Ironically, though, because these billions of dollars are largely pointed at boosting performance on narrow tests that do not measure or encourage the acquisition of higher-order skills, they do not result in the improvements to learning that would be possible if the same funds were spent differently.

HOW HIGH-QUALITY ASSESSMENTS CAN BE MADE AFFORDABLE

Earlier studies and cost estimates from current programs provide relatively similar estimates of the relatively higher costs of performance assessments in comparison to multiple-choice testing. For example, adjusted to current dollars,[4] cost estimates from several studies for development, administration, and scoring of assessment batteries that include significant performance components have ranged from about $30 to $50 per pupil, depending on how extensive the performance components are.[5] These estimates are mostly based on the practices used in the United States during the late 1980s and early 1990s. By comparison, a largely multiple-choice test costs about $20 to $25 per pupil to develop, administer, and score. A ratio of about 2 to 1 in terms of costs between performance-based and selected-response tests is also fairly constant across studies.

A 1993 General Accounting Office study highlighted potential cost savings based on the large spread in the cost of performance assessment, from $16 to $64 (with an average of $33). The upper estimates are mostly from studies of small-scale experiments using specialized materials and equipment (e.g., science kits) that had to be delivered to schools.[6] This spread suggests the potential for economies of scale and experience in developing and implementing performance assessments. When more students were included in test administrations, the study found that costs fell because the fixed costs were distributed over a larger number of students.

Previous research reported estimates for scoring individual performance tasks ranging from about $0.79 per student to over $8 per student, adjusted to current dollars (see table 6.1).[7] Costs variations are associated

Table 6.1 Scoring Time and Cost Estimates for Performance Assessments

Assessment	Scoring	Cost (converted to 2009 dollars)	Study
Connecticut Assessment of Educational Progress: 25-minute essay	Twice holistically (does not include staff costs for recruiting raters, procuring scoring sites, training table leaders, and selecting range finder papers and other categories)	$1.65 per student	Baron, 1984
Research study for SAT: 45-minute essay	Scored once holistically	$0.79 to $2.14 per student	Breland, Camp, Jones, Morris, & Rock, 1987
California Assessment Program: 45-minute essay	Scored twice	$7.29 per student	Hymes, 1991
College Board English Composition: 20-minute essay	Scored twice	$8.58 per student	Office of Technology Assessment, 1992
Geometry proofs	Not reported	$4.38 per student	Stevenson, 1990
Kentucky Assessment: On-demand tasks in a variety of subject areas	Total scoring time per student is 12 minutes	$4.38 per student	Hill & Reidy, 1993

Sources: Baron, J. B. (1984). Writing assessment in Connecticut: A holistic eye toward identification and an analytic eye toward instruction. *Educational Measurement: Issues and Practice,* *3,* 27–28, 38; Breland, H. M., Camp, R., Jones, R. J., Morris, M. M., & Rock, D. A. (1987). *Assessing writing skill.* New York, NY: College Entrance Examination Board; Hill, R., & Reidy, E. (1993). *The cost factors: Can performance based assessment be a sound investment?* Unpublished manuscript; Hymes, D. L. (1991). *The changing face of testing and assessment.* Arlington, VA: American Association of School Administrators; Stevenson, Z., Averett, C., & Vickers, D. (1990, April). *The reliability of using a focused-holistic scoring approach to measure student performance on a geometry proof.* Paper presented at the meeting of the American Educational Research Association, Boston, MA; Office of Technology Assessment. (1992). *Testing in American schools: Asking the right questions* (Report No. OTA-SET-519). Washington, DC: US Government Printing Office.

with the nature of the task, the number of scorers, and the costs categories included, among other things.

Using more comparable, contemporary data from a carefully grounded study by the Assessment Solutions Group (ASG) demonstrates that it is possible to construct affordable, large-scale assessment systems that include a significant number of constructed-response items, reliably scored classroom-based performance tasks, and traditional multiple-choice questions for no more than the cost of the much-less-informative systems used today.

Based on empirical cost data from multiple sources, the ASG study shows that such systems can be designed for no more than the costs paid by an average state for today's tests—generally about $25 per pupil for English language arts and math tests.[8] This can be accomplished by making sound decisions that take advantage of the economies of scale that can be achieved when states join together in testing consortia, with new uses of technology in distributing and scoring standardized tests, and with thoughtful approaches to using teachers in the scoring of performance items.

ASG developed cost models providing an apples-to-apples comparison for two types of tests: a typical summative multiple-choice test with primarily multiple-choice items and a high-quality assessment that includes more constructed response items and new item types, such as performance events (relatively short curriculum-embedded tasks) and more ambitious performance tasks. Table 6.2 shows the number of multiple-choice and extended-response items for each grade in a typical state test, alongside specifications for a new "high-quality" assessment (HQA), featuring a reduced number of multiple-choice items and the addition of performance tasks. The models are based on NCLB-testing requirements system (English language arts and mathematics tests in grades 3 to 8 and grade 10).

The high-quality assessment is assumed to include two performance events and one or two performance tasks, in addition to more constructed-response items. A distinction is drawn between performance events, in which an individual student writes a response in a summative testing situation, such as an extended writing prompt completed within one or two class periods, and performance tasks that involve more ambitious work,

Table 6.2 High-Quality Summative Assessment Design

Summative Assessment	Item Counts				
	Multiple Choice	Short Constructed Response (SCR)	Extended Constructed Response (ECR)	Performance Event	Performance Task
Mathematics					
Current typical assessment	50	0	2	0	0
High-quality assessment	25	2 (1 in grade 3)	2 (0 in grade 3, 1 in grade 4)	2	2 (0 in grade 3, 1 in grade 4)
English language arts					
Current typical assessment (reading)	50	0	2	0	0
Current typical assessment (writing)[a]	10	0	1	0	0
High-quality assessment (reading)	25	2 (1 in grades 3 and 4)	2 (1 in grades 3 and 4)	2	1
High-quality assessment (writing)[a]	10	2 (1 in grades 3 and 4)	2 (1 in grades 3 and 4)	2	0

[a]Administered in grades 4, 7, and 10.

such as a research project in which students prepare a paper and make a presentation. In the latter case, the assessment costs include developing the curriculum and materials to scaffold student progress throughout the task, as well as allowing more scoring time.

This model estimates that a current multiple-choice testing battery in a typical state—including both reading and mathematics tests, plus benchmark or interim testing—costs around $50 per pupil. In the same typical state, the HQA, including the same subjects and benchmark assessments, would cost around $55 per pupil before cost-reduction strategies are applied. When such strategies are applied, the cost of performance assessments drops significantly—in the best case, to below $20 per pupil (see figure 6.2).

The strategies include:

- *Participation in a consortium.* The model includes state consortium sizes of ten, twenty, and thirty states. The use of a state consortium reduces costs by an average of $15 per pupil. The consortium approach represents a significant decrease in assessment cost.

- *Uses of technology.* Computers are used for online test delivery, to distribute human scoring of some of the open-ended items, and for automated scoring for certain constructed response items. Together these innovations account for cost savings of about $3 to $4 per pupil and are likely to provide more reductions as efficiencies are developed in programming and using technology for these purposes.

- *Two approaches to the use of teacher-moderated scoring.* Teacher-moderated scoring can net both substantial cost reductions and the potential professional development benefits already discussed. ASG estimates two models for teacher-moderated scoring, one a professional development model with no additional teacher compensation beyond that supported by the state or district for normal professional development days and the other assuming a $125 per day stipend to teachers. These strategies for using teachers as scorers reduce costs by an additional $10 to $20 per pupil, depending on whether teachers are paid or engaged as part of professional development. (See table 6.3.)

If all possible cost-saving strategies are combined, the per-pupil cost for the high-quality assessment is just under $15 per pupil in a thirty-state consortium, less than the estimated cost of the typical summative state test. Paying teachers a stipend to score increases this cost to about $25 per pupil, about the same amount paid for the typical multiple-choice testing battery a student takes today. The estimated time for scoring, based on contemporary evidence about teacher scoring time on similar tasks, decreases as scorers become more highly skilled.

Indeed, the two multistate assessment consortia that are developing assessments of the Common Core State Standards, which include

Figure 6.2

Diminishing Expenditures per Capita for High-Quality Assessments

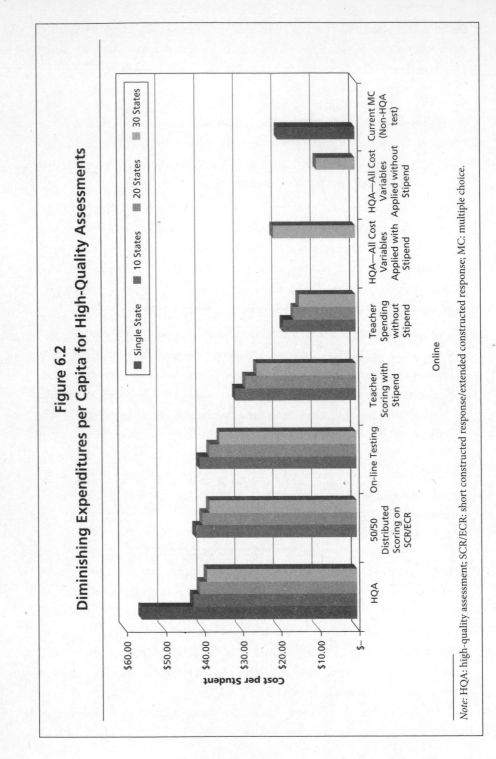

Note: HQA: high-quality assessment; SCR/ECR: short constructed response/extended constructed response; MC: multiple choice.

Table 6.3 Assessment Costs under Different Teacher Scoring Assumptions

Consortium Size	Contractor Cost (On-Site Scoring)	Teacher Stipend ($125)	Teacher Professional Development Scoring
10 states	$42.41	$31.17	$18.70
30 states	$38.83	$25.71	$14.57

constructed responses and performance tasks, have estimated the costs of their systems at $23 to $29 for the summative tests. For the Smarter Balanced Assessment Consortium, a system that also includes formative tools and interim assessments is expected to cost states about $27 per pupil.

Ultimately a state could score assessments with the features included in these new systems by underwriting about two professional development days per teacher in the relevant subject areas. Whether incorporated into professional development costs or paid directly through stipends, teacher involvement in scoring is not only useful in making performance assessments affordable, it is also critical, as we have seen, in supporting instruction aimed at higher-order thinking and performance skills.

A COST-BENEFIT PERSPECTIVE

A legitimate concern in designing assessment systems has been the cost of using performance tasks that meet the requirements of valid and reliable assessment, as we have outlined them earlier. Of course, costs for tests themselves are not the only important information for making an economically and educationally wise decision. Opportunity costs and benefits of assessment decisions are also important to consider. For example, studies have documented important opportunity costs of widely used tests in the United States. Among these is evidence that high-stakes tests that are narrowly focused on basic skills evaluated in a multiple-choice format reduce emphasis on strategies that support transferable learning, such as research, inquiry, and applications of knowledge to a variety of contexts, extended writing and defense of ideas, and development of higher-order thinking skills.[9]

In addition, current testing systems provide very little textured information to help teachers improve learning: the tests deliver scores rather than evidence of student work that can be closely examined and understood in terms of a learning continuum for specific skills. They reveal little of students' thinking, reasoning, and misconceptions, and almost nothing about their actual performance beyond the bounds of recognizing or guessing answers in items where they are already supplied.

Costs associated with a comprehensive assessment system are reflected in both money and time. Because the time used for current testing and test preparation often does little to help students acquire transferable knowledge and skills, teachers often feel it is "lost" to instruction rather than that it reflects, supports, and reinforces instruction. Data in the form of scores is supplied months after students have left school for the summer. Thus, the opportunity costs of current tests are fairly high, and they produce relatively few benefits in terms of expanded knowledge about important student learning for students and teachers.

From a cost-benefit perspective, the current approach is penny wise and pound foolish. Although they may appear low in costs, today's testing programs are generally not organized to produce the benefits of deeper student learning found in high-performing countries. Instead we have a set of fragmented, disjointed efforts, unable to measure the most important learning goals, and not useful to teachers' efforts to understand how their students think and what can be done to support their success.

On the flip side of these opportunity costs are the potential benefits of using a performance assessment system that is information rich in the ways that we have described. While the development, use, and scoring of performance tasks does require time and expertise, educators and policymakers in virtually all high-achieving nations believe that the value of rich performance assessments far outweighs their cost. Many countries have expanded their use of performance tasks because these deeply engage teachers and students in learning, make rigorous and cognitively demanding instruction commonplace, and, policymakers have argued, will likely increase students' achievement levels and readiness for college and careers.

The costs of performance assessment are also accompanied by the benefits of giving teachers incentives and skills to engage in more ambitious kinds of teaching and more rigorous assignments in the classroom, more feedback about student thinking and performance, and models for crafting their own assessments, which can lead to stronger instruction and learning.

In these respects, performance assessment is a Trojan horse for instructional reform. As policy analyst Milbrey McLaughlin has noted, "It is exceedingly difficult for policy to change practice. . . . Change ultimately is a problem of the smallest unit."[10] Approaches to assessment that include teacher-scored, curriculum-embedded tasks reach into classrooms to stimulate change for teachers and students. By engaging teachers in the development, use, and scoring of these assessments, teachers can develop a shared conception of high-quality instruction over time and through practice. They can internalize what counts as evidence of high-quality student work. Teachers and administrators can develop knowledge of high-quality assessment design principles and of how assessment should inform curriculum and instruction. They can also see firsthand which instructional patterns lead to particular characteristics of a performance.

The investment of resources for assessment-based scoring and professional development might be viewed as an opportunity to use professional development resources more wisely. The one-shot flavor-of-the-month workshops that still constitute the bulk of American professional development leverage less knowledge and change in practice than engagement in developing and scoring assessments has been found to yield.[11] A coherent assessment system could redirect a portion of professional development dollars toward more meaningful use, focused tightly on student learning, and create a paradigm shift about how to organize teachers' learning to support more effective instruction.

Finally, the engagement of educators in assessment development can also enable assessment designers to create more valid, reliable, and fair assessments, because they gain finely grained information about the contexts in which the assessments are used.

While looking to economize, it is also important to put the costs of high-quality assessment into perspective. While working in a consortium, using technology, and combining cost-effective approaches to computer-based and teacher scoring would put the costs of such a system in the range of $25 to $30 per student, the costs of other instructional interventions are much greater. For example, a study of three comprehensive school reform models (with modest impact on achievement) found that spending on professional development averaged almost $600 per pupil.[12] In the context of a tightly integrated teaching and learning system, the use of performance assessment may offer an important and much more cost-effective method for influencing instructional practice.

chapter 7

Building Systems of Assessment

As we noted earlier, performance assessments can and should be used within a system of assessments that takes into account the varied needs of constituents who use assessment data. These include students, parents, and teachers; principals, superintendents, and boards of education; postsecondary officials and administrators in both colleges and career-technical programs; employers; state education department staff, legislators, and governors; the business community; and many others.

A system of assessments does not rely on a single source of data; rather, it creates a strategic mix of information that provides a more holistic picture of students, schools, and educational systems. It also supports high-quality learning opportunities by giving more actionable information for teaching and school planning and by encouraging the kind of teaching and learning students need to succeed as independent actors.

No one test, however innovative it may be, can hope to address all, or even most, of the variables that matter for college and career readiness and for success in life. More important, many of these need to be measured in low-stakes contexts, with feedback provided to students on where they stand relative to their goals, not with the intent of classifying them or withholding a benefit, such as access to a particular program, curriculum, or diploma.

Here, for example, are a number of important Common Core standards that, due to their very nature, cannot be directly measured by the consortia assessments:

- Conducting extended research using multiple forms of evidence
- Communicating ideas orally, graphically, and in writing
- Presenting data and ideas in multimedia formats
- Collaborating with others to define or solve a problem
- Planning, evaluating, and refining solution strategies
- Using mathematical tools and models in science, technology, and engineering contexts

It is easy to see that many of these standards are critical to college and career readiness. It is also readily apparent that these standards require a wider range of assessment techniques, many of which will work best in a classroom environment. For example, the standard for planning, evaluating, and refining solution strategies suggests a multistep process where evidence is generated at multiple points in the process. Designing and using mathematical models is a task that occurs most naturally in other subject areas, such as the natural and social sciences, and engineering, through complex problems set in real-world contexts.

The rich instructional experiences and products that result from such efforts should be available to inform teaching and student improvement rather than merely producing scores that are determined outside the school and sent back in as two-digit numbers that reveal little about what students have actually accomplished. Although these products can and should inform summative judgments, they should also serve formative purposes—helping teachers understand student thinking and performance and helping students understand how they can continue to revise and improve their work. Systems of assessment can allow various elements to be used for different purposes, creating more transparency and utility than a single secure test can offer.

WHAT DO SYSTEMS OF ASSESSMENT CONSIST OF?

Systems of assessment are designed strategically to offer information for distinctive purposes to different audiences: students, parents, teachers, administrators, and policymakers at the classroom, school, district, and state levels. A system of assessment may include large-scale assessments that offer information to policymakers (these are sometimes conducted on a sampling basis rather than for each student), along with much richer school or classroom assessments that offer more detailed information to guide teachers as they develop curriculum and instruction and students as they revise their work and set learning goals.

Colleges and employers can benefit from both summary data (e.g., grade point averages or test scores) and, in certain circumstances, more complex and authentic examples of students' work such as essays or other writing samples, work products students have designed or fashioned, and presentations that showcase their thinking.

In its description of its new assessment framework, New Hampshire's Department of Education notes:

> Comprehensive assessment systems are generally defined as multiple levels of assessment designed to provide information for different users to fulfill different purposes. Most importantly, information gathered from classroom and school assessments should provide information to supplement accountability information generated at the state level, and state level assessments should provide information useful for evaluating local education programs and informing instructional practice. Further, the large-scale assessment should signal the kinds of learning expectations coherent with the intent of the standards and the kinds of learning demonstrations we would like to see in classrooms.[1]

A key point in New Hampshire's approach is that large-scale assessments should signal important learning goals and be compatible with the kinds of teaching that are desired in classrooms, and they should work in tandem with local assessments to meet information needs.

Examples of State Systems

Current testing regimes in most states lack this kind of coherence and synergy and fail to measure deeper learning skills. However, a number of states developed thoughtful systems of assessment during the 1990s. These standards-based systems of curriculum and assessment included large-scale, on-demand tests in a number of subject areas—usually once in each grade span (3–5, 6–8, 9–12), plus classroom-based assessments that involved students in completing performance tasks, such as science investigations; research, writing, or art projects; and including portfolios of student work assembled over time to illustrate specific competencies.

The on-demand tests usually included a combination of multiple-choice and short constructed-response items, with longer essays to evaluate writing. These scores informed state and local policymakers about how students were doing overall in key areas. Some states, including Connecticut, Maine, Maryland, New York, and Vermont, involved students in classroom performance tasks of longer duration—from one class period to several—designed at the state level and administered and scored locally, with a moderated scoring process to ensure consistency. Maryland was able to mount an ambitious set of tasks across subject areas by using matrix sampling, which meant that different groups of students completed different tasks, and the results could be aggregated across a district or the state to report on more aspects of learning culled from across all the tasks.

Minnesota, Oregon, Wisconsin, and Wyoming introduced more individualized learning profiles of students that allowed students to demonstrate specified competencies through locally developed performance assessments. Minnesota's Profiles of Learning set out expectations for graduation readiness in ten domains not tested in the state's basic skills tests. For example, in social studies, the inquiry standard could be met with an issue analysis that required the student to research an issue and evaluate proposed positions or solutions by gathering information on the issue, evaluating points of view, looking for areas of difference and agreement, analyzing feasibility and practicality for proposed solutions, and comparing alternatives and their projected consequences. Oregon's Certificates of Initial and Advanced Mastery included similar tasks that students could complete to demonstrate their competencies in various areas. These could then be recorded on the diploma. Students could use these competency demonstrations to meet proficiency-based entrance requirements at Oregon's public universities.

Graduation portfolios in states like Rhode Island and New York have taken this idea a step further. All districts in Rhode Island have developed portfolios for graduation to illustrate accomplishment of a range of deeper learning skills. Schools in the New York Performance Standards Consortium, described earlier, have received a state-approved waiver allowing their students to complete a graduation portfolio in lieu of most of the state Regents Examinations. This portfolio includes a set of ambitious performance tasks—a scientific investigation, a mathematical model, a literary analysis, and a history/social science research paper, sometimes augmented with other tasks like an arts demonstration or analyses of a community service or internship experience. These meet common standards and are evaluated on common scoring rubrics. New Hampshire introduced a technology portfolio for graduation, which allows students to collect evidence to show how they have met standards in this field.

Although NCLB led to the marginalization of many of these elements from accountability reports, coherent systems of assessment have long existed in a number of other countries. Examination systems in England, Singapore, and Australia, for example, have common features that can also be found in the International Baccalaureate system. Students typically choose the subjects or courses of study in which they will take examinations to demonstrate their competence or qualifications, based on their interests and strengths. These qualifications exams are offered in vocational subjects as well as traditional academic subjects. Part of the exam grade is based on externally developed, "sit-down" tests that feature open-ended essays and problems; the remainder, which can range from 25 to 60 percent of the total score, is based on specific tasks undertaken in the classroom to meet syllabus requirements. (See chapter 3.)

These classroom-based assessments are generally created by the examinations board and are scored by local teachers according to common rubrics in a moderation process that ensures consistency in scoring. They may range from a portfolio-like collection of assignments, like the tasks required for England's General Certificate of Secondary Education exam in English, to single large projects that complement the sit-down test, like the science investigation required as part of Singapore's high school science examinations.

Queensland, Australia, offers a useful example of how the elements of a system come together (see table 7.1). In Queensland, national testing

Table 7.1 Queensland's System of Assessments

	Presecondary Level	Senior Level (grades 11–12)
Curriculum guidance	Essential Learnings: Scope and sequence guides, unit templates, plus assessable elements and quality descriptors (rubrics)	Syllabi for each subject outlining content and assessments
External tests	National tests of literacy and numeracy at grades 3, 5, 7; centrally scored	Queensland Core Skills Test, grade 12
Locally administered performance tasks	Queensland Comparable Assessment Tasks (QCAT): Common performance tasks at grades 4, 6, and 9; locally scored	Course assessments, outlined in syllabus; locally scored and externally moderated
Locally developed assessments	Local performance assessment systems; locally scored and externally moderated	Graduation portfolios; locally scored and externally moderated

occurs at grades 3, 5, 7, and 9, and the state offers a reference exam at grade 12. Most assessment is conducted through common statewide performance tasks that are administered locally, plus a rich system of local performance assessments developed at the school level but subject to quality control and moderation of scoring by a state panel. The Queensland Curriculum, Assessment, and Reporting Framework (QCAR) helps provide consistency from school to school based on the state's content standards, called Essential Learnings, which include unit templates and guidance for assessments in each subject. These include extended research projects, analyses, and problem solutions across fields.

The kinds of performance tasks required in the system reflect the learning progressions along which students are expected to develop over time. They are also intended to develop students' abilities to guide their own learning, which become more sophisticated as they have repeated opportunities to engage complex tasks and their teachers learn to incorporate this kind of work into the curriculum. For example, in exhibit 7.1, we show a common task used in grade 7 in science and one expected of students at the senior level. The tasks illustrate students' learning progression from being able to carry out an investigation defined for them to being able to conduct a much more complex investigation that they initiate and design themselves.

Exhibit 7.1 Queensland Science Assessments at Grades 7 and Senior Level

Task QCAT for Seventh-Grade Science

90 minutes over 1–2 days. Given some contextual information, students must analyze and construct food webs in two environments. Through multiple prompts, students must show an understanding of food chains and the impact of environmental disruptions on populations.

Extended Experimental Investigation at the Senior Level, Grades 11–12

Over four or more weeks, students must develop and conduct an extended experimental investigation to investigate a hypothesis or to answer a practical research question. Experiments may be laboratory or field based. The outcome of the investigation is a written scientific report of 1500 to 2000 words.
    The student must:

- develop a planned course of action
- clearly articulate the research question and provide a statement of purpose for the investigation
- provide descriptions of the experiment
- show evidence of student design
- provide evidence of primary and secondary data collection and selection
- execute the experiment(s)
- analyze data
- discuss the outcomes of the experiment
- evaluate and justify conclusion(s).

Source: Conley, D. T., & Darling-Hammond, L. (2013). *Creating systems of assessment for deeper learning.* Stanford, CA: Stanford Center for Opportunity Policy in Education.

The Role of Teachers

Another important aspect of a system of assessment is that it supports an integrated teaching and learning system. By routinely engaging teachers in developing, scoring, and debriefing assessments so that they can learn from the results, such a system links assessment to curriculum, teaching, and teacher development. In the Queensland case, groups of teachers within schools develop, administer, and score the assessments with reference to the national curriculum guidelines and state syllabi (also developed by teachers). At the high school level, a student's work is collected into a portfolio that is used as the primary measure of college readiness. Portfolio scoring is moderated by panels that include teachers from other schools and professors from the higher education system. A statewide examination serves as an external validity check, but not as the accountability measure for individual students.

This type of assessment can be used as a reliable and valid measure because over time, educators have acquired very similar ideas of what adequate performance on these papers and tasks looks like. In nations as varied as the Netherlands and Singapore, these shared mental models of student performance on tasks shape teacher judgments. These are developed from the earliest stages of teacher education and are reinforced by high-quality in-course assessments and grading practices based on scoring guides that are closely aligned with standards.

In such systems, the combination of training, moderated scoring, and auditing has allowed performance assessments to be scored at high levels of reliability while offering a valid method for evaluating higher-order skills. Where school systems have devoted resources to assessment at the classroom level and have invested in classroom-based performance assessors, teachers have developed deep expertise that translates into shared judgments and common mental models of what constitutes acceptable student performance on complex types of learning.

Furthermore, when teachers become experienced in developing and evaluating high-quality performance assessments, they are better able to design and deliver high-quality learning experiences because they have a stronger understanding of what kinds of tasks elicit thoughtful work, how students think as they complete such tasks, and what a quality standard looks like. Both teachers and students gain insights into how students learn in the specific content area and how, as a team, they can facilitate improvements in this learning.

Because performance assessments model worthwhile tasks and expectations, embed assessment into the curriculum, and develop teachers' understanding of how to interpret and respond to student learning, their use typically improves instruction. Learning is also strengthened as students are able to work on these assessment tasks intensively, revise them to meet standards, and display their learning to parents, peers, teachers, and even future professors and employers. Policymakers are able to track general trends as scores from multiple measures are aggregated, reported, and analyzed.

HOW CAN ASSESSMENT BE MADE USEFUL FOR STUDENTS?

Assessment can be instructive. While most would agree with this in principle, in practice, we tend to create a distinction between teaching and testing. Students can learn a great deal from assessments beyond where they stand in comparison to other students or the teacher's expectations as expressed in a grade or a test score.

Assessment to Guide Learning

A primary, though often forgotten, purpose of high-quality assessments is to help students learn how to improve their own work and learning strategies. Particularly in this era when learning-to-learn skills are increasingly important, it is critical that assessments help students internalize standards, become better able to reflect on and evaluate their own work, and be motivated and capable of revising and improving it, as well as seeking out additional resources (human and otherwise) to answer emerging questions.

Assessments can serve these purposes when they are clearly linked to standards that are reflected in the rubrics used for scoring the work, when their criteria are made available to students as they are developing their work, and when students are given the opportunity to engage in self- and peer assessments using these tools. In addition, students develop these skills when assessments ask them to exhibit their work in presentations to others, where they must both explain their ideas or solutions and answer questions that probe more deeply, and then revise the work to address these further questions.

Through the use of rubrics and public presentations, students can receive feedback that is precise, as well as generalizable. They end up with a much better idea of what to do differently next time—one that is far more useful than what they might infer from an item analysis on a standardized test or generalized comments from a teacher on a paper such as "nice job," or "good point." When students receive feedback of many different types from different sources, they begin to triangulate among them to identify patterns of strength and weakness beyond just the specific questions they got right or wrong. This more comprehensive, holistic sense of knowledge and skills empowers the learner and builds self-awareness and self-efficacy.

This approach to assessment assumes that students are a primary consumer of the information they produce, and it designs assessment processes that explicitly develop students' metacognitive skills and give them opportunities for reflection and revision to meet standards. Not incidentally, these processes also support student learning by deepening teachers' understanding of what constitutes high-quality work and how to support it both individually and collectively as a staff.

Assessment to Construct Student Profiles

Assessments can also support student learning by giving an overview of what students have accomplished, thus pointing to areas where students can take pride and further develop their strengths—with an eye toward college and career pursuits—as well as areas where they need to focus for further development.

Information from a range of sources can be combined into a student profile, which provides additional data, such as teacher observations and ratings of students, student self-reports, and other measures such as internships and public service experiences. The profile is different from a transcript because it contains a wider range of information and because, where possible, it presents the information in relation to student aspirations and interests. In other words, students who wish to pursue health occupations would have evidence in their profile of the degree to which they are developing the knowledge and skills needed to enter this general field of study and pursue a career in it. Knowing something about student interests and aspirations provides a lens through which profile data can be interpreted and readiness determinations made more precisely. The profile can, of course, also include information about readiness in relation to the requirements of general education courses at different kinds of two- and four-year institutions.

A profile approach is important in part because students can be expected to perform only as highly as their aspirations dictate. Getting students to engage in challenging learning tasks requires that they have some motivation or reason for doing so. A profile connected to interests and aspirations helps show students why it is important to strive to achieve academically and what they can profitably focus on to enable them to pursue their own goals. Profiles go a step beyond some current college admissions processes that rely largely on grades and admissions tests scores. More selective schools already review a wider array of data that constitutes a profile. The admissions process seeks to learn more about student interests and aspirations and how these align with their preparation. This process is often called portfolio review. Why only the highest-achieving students should be encouraged to form and pursue goals is not at all clear, especially at a time when all students are being urged to raise their expectations and engage more deeply in cognitively challenging learning.

Gathering and reporting information in this fashion is consistent with a research-based model of college and career readiness and leads to a full portrait of the knowledge, skills, and dispositions students need to succeed after high school. The profile provides students a clear read on the degree to which they are ready to pursue their postsecondary goals and also signals to teachers and schools a wider range of areas where student readiness needs to be addressed. While this information might be less useful for some high-stakes accountability purposes, it is absolutely essential for students to have as they seek to become ready for their futures.

A sample profile (intended to be illustrative only) could have the following types of measures in it:

- Common Core State Standards consortia exams
- Grade point average (cumulative and disaggregated by subject)
- Admissions tests (e.g., SAT, ACT) or sequence of Common Core or admissions-aligned tests (e.g., Aspire, Pathways)
- Classroom-administered performance tasks (e.g., research papers)
- Oral presentation beyond consortia requirements, scored discussion

- Teacher rating of student note-taking skills, ability to follow directions, persistence with challenging tasks, and other evidence of learning skills and ownership of learning
- Student self-report on effort used to complete an activity and student self-report of actions taken to achieve personal goals
- Student self-report of college or career aspirations and goals
- Student postsecondary plans

This list ranges from standardized tests to challenging performance assessments and self-reports of plans, goals, and actions. Although the measures are not comparable and cannot be combined into a single score, they are useful precisely because they offer insights into different aspects of a student's abilities and goals.

Regardless of the precise measures selected to comprise it, a profile approach will serve as clearer guidance to students about where they stand in relation to college and career readiness around their specific goals. They can then act to change their behavior consistent with their goals. Student ownership of learning is strengthened by attention to a wider range of behavior and skills that values their aspirations. Postsecondary institutions receive much more actionable information that they can use to improve student success, while state agencies and other stakeholders get a truer picture of how well schools are preparing students for college and careers.

Assessment to Inform Valid Decisions

Whenever a decision is being made about an individual student, the information used must be valid and able to support the inference being made about what a student can do or benefit from. The tendency to make decisions based on the results of a test cut score may be a convenient way to report certain kinds of data (e.g., how many students have achieved a particular level of performance), but it is inappropriate for making a consequential decision about a student. The Standards for Educational and Psychological Testing make it clear that using a cut score on a single assessment to make a high-stakes decision is a violation of a number of principles of good test design and appropriate score use.[2]

The higher the stakes are at the individual level, the more information is needed to understand a student's knowledge and capacity. For example, if scores are going to be used to make decisions about graduation, remediation, program placement, admissions, or financial aid, more than a single test score is required. Additional sources of information on the knowledge and skills associated with readiness and success allow for more accurate interpretation based on evidence about the individual. Such data, including classroom-based performance evidence, are important to reduce the probability of making incorrect status determinations.

A system of assessments can provide the valid, reliable information needed for a variety of purposes, including important educational decisions. In fact, college admission at most four-year institutions in the United States already takes multiple data sources into account, combining grade point averages with information about a student's course work choices, extracurricular experiences, test scores, essays, and sometimes interviews. In some cases where a student is on the margin, additional information from the application or a portfolio of work may be examined before a decision is made.

HOW MIGHT STATES DEVELOP SYSTEMS OF ASSESSMENT?

A system-of-assessments approach opens the door to a much wider array of measurement instruments and approaches. Currently states limit their assessment options because almost all assessment is viewed through the lens of high-stakes accountability purposes and the technical requirements associated with these types of tests. This makes sense as far as it goes, but current assessments are not sufficient to bring about improvements in student readiness for college and careers because readiness depends on more than what is measured by high-stakes tests. A system of assessments yields a wider range of actionable information that students and their teachers can use to develop the broad range of knowledge and skills needed for postsecondary success.

As states seek to develop such systems, they should consider how to meet the needs of various stakeholders for useful information, beginning with students themselves—along with their teachers and families who support their learning—and extending to policymakers who need to know how to invest in instructional improvements at the school, district, and state level. In addition, employers and institutions of higher education need to understand what students know and can do as they leave high school and enter college or the workplace. Critically important is that this information be meaningful for these purposes rather than a remote proxy and that it encourages productive instruction truly supportive of deeper learning that students will be able to transfer to new situations.

As they seek to develop new systems of assessment, states should:

- Define college and career readiness
- Evaluate the gap between the system as it now exists and the desired system
- Identify policy purposes for state and local assessments
- Consider a continuum of assessments that address different purposes
- Identify the information assessments need to generate for different users:
  o Policymakers (state and local)
  o Students and parents
  o Teachers
  o Higher education and employers
- Develop assessments that can provide a profile of student abilities and accomplishments
- Connect these assessments to curriculum, instruction, and professional development in a productive teaching and learning system
- Create an accountability system that encourages the kinds of learning and practice that are needed to reach the goals of college and career readiness.

An example of one state's well-considered approach to developing such a system is the plan currently under way in New Hampshire (see exhibit 7.2).

Exhibit 7.2 Designing a System of Assessments in New Hampshire

To ensure its students' preparation for college and careers, New Hampshire has begun to create a system of assessments that is tightly connected to curriculum, instruction, and professional learning. In addition to the Smarter Balanced Assessments in English language arts and mathematics, this system will include a set of common performance tasks that have high technical quality in the core academic subjects, locally designed assessments with guidelines for ensuring quality, regional scoring sessions and local district peer review audits to ensure sound accountability systems and interrater reliability, a web-based bank of local and common performance tasks, and a network of practitioner "assessment experts" to support schools.

The state's view is that a well-developed system of performance assessments that augment the traditional tests will drive improvements in teaching and learning, as they "promote the use of authentic, inquiry-based instruction, complex thinking, and application of learning . . . [and] incentivize the type of instruction and assessment that support student learning of rich knowledge and skills." The system will also offer a strategic approach for building the expertise of educators across the state by organizing professional development around the design, implementation, and scoring of these assessments, which model good instruction and provide insights about teaching and learning.

Assessment information gathered from the local assessment system, including common and locally developed performance tasks, is expected to provide the bulk of the information used for school, educator, and student accountability systems. Meanwhile, the large-scale assessment system will provide information to support school accountability determinations and, perhaps, supplement educator accountability determinations. To accomplish this, over three years (from 2013 to 2015), the state will:

- Develop college- and career-ready *competencies* reflecting higher-order thinking and performance skills for the core disciplines of English language arts, math, science, social studies, and the arts.
- Use these competencies to guide the development of *common statewide performance tasks* in each of these content areas at each grade span (K–5, 6–8, 9–12), with accompanying guidelines, tools, rubrics, student work anchors, and data reporting. Each task will be constructed as a

(Continued)

(Continued)

complex, multistep, curriculum-embedded assignment that measures the depth and application of student learning.

- Develop a process, tools, and protocols for supporting districts and schools in developing and validating high-quality *local performance tasks*, along with guidance for teachers in how to use these to strengthen curriculum and instruction.
- Assemble both the common and locally developed tasks into a *web-based bank* of validated performance tasks to be used for formative as well as summative assessments.
- Organize *professional development institutes* for cohorts of schools focused on the design, validation, and reliable scoring of tasks, as well as data analysis to track student progress and inform instruction.
- Create *regional support networks* led by practitioner assessment experts to help build capacity in schools and support regional task validation and calibration scoring sessions, with a goal of 80 percent or greater interrater reliability on locally scored tasks.
- Maintain technical quality and consistency through *district peer review audits*, in which districts will submit evidence of their performance assessment systems to peer review teams of external practitioners, who will review the evidence based on common criteria, including whether the district has developed.

A key part of the accountability system, these audits will examine how districts administer common and local tasks, manage a quality assurance process, develop educators' skills, and design policies and practices that support the state performance assessment system (e.g., performance-based graduation requirements).

New Hampshire and other states that work to produce more useful and informative assessments are endeavoring to integrate assessment with teaching and learning. As more open-ended tasks offer more information about how students think and perform, they are also more useful for formative purposes, although they can and should offer information for summative judgments as well. In a new system of assessment, we should be able to move from an overemphasis on entirely external summative tests to a greater emphasis on assessment that can shape and inform learning. (See figure 7.1.)

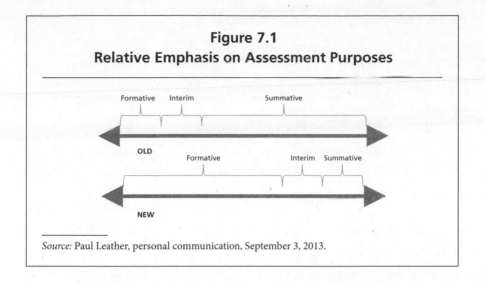

Figure 7.1

Relative Emphasis on Assessment Purposes

Formative   Interim   Summative

OLD

Formative   Interim   Summative

NEW

Source: Paul Leather, personal communication, September 3, 2013.

HOW SHOULD ACCOUNTABILITY SYSTEMS EVOLVE?

As states develop new systems of assessment, it will be important to develop new systems of accountability as well. As they do so, it is important to incorporate productive uses of new assessments while recognizing that assessments of student performance provide information for an accountability system, but they are not the system itself.

Genuine accountability can occur only when useful processes exist for using information to improve what schools and teachers do on behalf of students.[3] Assessments and outcome standards alone cannot guarantee that schools will know how to improve or be able to make the changes that will help students learn more effectively. In fact, if such standards are improperly designed, they can undermine accountability.

Accountability for education is achieved when the policies and practices of a school, district, and state work both to provide quality education and to correct problems as they occur. Assessment data are helpful to the extent that they provide relevant, valid, and timely information about how individual students are doing and how schools are serving them. But these kinds of data are only a small part of the total process. An accountability system is a set of commitments, policies, and practices that are designed to:

1. Increase the probability that schools will use good practices on behalf of students

2. Reduce the likelihood that schools will engage in harmful practices

3. Encourage ongoing assessment on the part of schools and educators to identify, diagnose, and change courses of action that are harmful or ineffective

Thus, in addition to outcome standards that rely on many kinds of data, accountability must encompass *professional standards of practice*—how a school, school system, or state ensures that the best available knowledge will be used to design schools and teach students through its hiring, professional development, and evaluation processes, as well as its processes for developing curriculum, assessing students, and engaging in continual improvement. These core building blocks of accountability reveal the capacity of educational institutions to serve their students well.

Even with the advent of more challenging and authentic measures of student performance, the creation of accountable schools and school systems will demand methods for inspiring *equitable access to appropriate learning opportunities* so that all students can achieve these learning goals. A complete view of accountability must take into account the appropriate roles of states and school districts in supporting local schools in their efforts to meet standards. This includes *accountability for resources*.

Accountability tools must address the barriers to good education that exist not only within schools and classrooms, but at the district, state, and national levels as well. Although schools themselves may be appropriately viewed as the unit of change in education reform, the structuring of inequality in learning opportunities occurs outside the school in the governmental units where funding formulas, resource allocations, and other educational policies are forged. In sum, if students are to be well served, accountability must be reciprocal. That is, federal, state, and local education agencies must themselves meet certain standards of delivery while school-based educators and students are expected to meet certain standards of practice and learning.

Finally, accountability for meaningful learning should be based on:

- *High-quality assessments* that encourage and reflect deeper learning and authentic evidence of student readiness to succeed in college and in work.
- *Profiles of information* about students, teachers, schools, and districts that move beyond a single cut score to a richer set of data that can provide indicators of accomplishment and grist for ongoing improvement.
- *Multiple measures* that are complementary and contribute to a comprehensive picture of the quality of learning in classrooms, schools, school systems, and states. These should be used in thoughtful systems of judgment to inform decision making at each level. Like businesses that use a dashboard of measures to provide a comprehensive picture of performance, we need to allow and enable accountability systems that create dashboards of indicators for all key decisions (student placement, promotion, graduation; teacher evaluation, tenure, dismissal; school recognition, intervention).

In the context of a comprehensive system of accountability, a system of assessments should strive to recognize and acknowledge that education is a complex process and that meeting goals for students, teachers, and schools requires indicators that draw from direct measures of the actual knowledge and skills associated with subsequent success. Most important, all of the elements of a system of assessments should be actionable and under the control of educators to improve. The more directly educators can address the accountability measures and effect changes in student behavior associated with them, the more likely they are to do so.

chapter 8

Conclusion

Performance assessments have been an integral part of educational systems in most high-achieving countries and some states in the United States. Evidence suggests that the nature and format of assessments affect the depth of knowledge and types of skills developed by students and that performance assessments are better suited to assessing high-level, complex thinking skills. Such assessments are also more likely to encourage the acquisition of such skills. Furthermore, there is evidence that engaging teachers in these assessments can strengthen curriculum and instruction and support more diagnostic teaching practices.

Our review suggests that large-scale testing in the United States could be improved by the thoughtful incorporation of well-constructed performance assessments that can represent higher-order, cognitively demanding performance standards; provide clearer signals to teachers about the kinds of student performances that are valued; and reduce pressures to mimic multiple-choice teaching in classroom instruction.

Much has been learned about how to develop, administer, and score performance tasks so that they provide valid, reliable, and fair evidence of student knowledge and skills and so that they can engage teachers productively without creating overwhelming burdens. New systems of assessment will benefit from incorporating these practices, along with new uses of technology to reduce costs and increase efficiencies by distributing and administering assessments, enabling new kinds of simulations and tasks, and strategically supporting both machine and human scoring.

There are costs and benefits associated with testing for accountability in whatever form that testing takes. We are used to the current high-stakes, multiple-choice model, but that does not mean it is cost free or benefit rich. Incorporating performance assessments into testing systems will pose some trade-offs, and we are more likely to make wise decisions if we understand these trade-offs more fully.

In general, the addition of performance tasks will increase the overall cost of assessment. However, costs can be reduced significantly—to levels comparable to current spending on tests—if states join together in consortia, use technology wisely, create and score tasks in efficient ways, and involve teachers in scoring. If teachers' participation is conceptualized as part of their ongoing professional development, costs can be reduced even further and benefits for instruction can be increased.

Research has documented how the use of common standards-based performance assessments that are designed and collaboratively evaluated by teachers can have many benefits, including these:

- Providing teachers with more direct and valid information about student progress than is offered by traditional assessments, especially on the deeper learning skills that characterize the Common Core State Standards

- Enabling teachers to engage in evidence-based work and reflecting more clearly and analytically on student work to inform their instructional decisions

- Yielding information that enhances teachers' knowledge of students, standards, curriculum, and teaching, especially when scoring is combined with debriefing and discussing next steps with other teachers

Furthermore, the cost of even the most performance-rich assessment system imaginable is dwarfed by other spending on education—spending often increased in response to impoverished learning outcomes when high-quality tests are not in use. Even if states spent fifty dollars per pupil on assessments (more than twice our estimate of the costs of a balanced system), this would still be less than half of 1 percent of average education spending. Given the power of assessment to change practice and guide learning and the opportunity costs of the current approach, such an investment is minuscule relative to its potential benefits.

While standards and assessments provide teachers and students with explanations of and access to images of excellence, this awareness is not sufficient. Adequate supports also need to be provided to build the capacities of all teachers and students to achieve these new and more challenging standards. Special attention and resources need to be allocated to provide teachers and students, especially those in historically underserved communities, with the appropriate opportunities to learn so that they can be sufficiently prepared to reach higher levels of success.

This capacity building is the central requirement of a truly accountable system. States interested in pursuing a system of assessments within a productive approach to accountability should consider the following steps:

1. *Define college and career readiness comprehensively*, noting what will be involved with measuring all the components of the definition and supporting students to meet these goals.

- Realign other policy areas, program requirements, and funding to these goals, so that the state has a focused system of efforts that pulls in a common direction.

- Identify the information that is needed to determine if students are college and career ready based on this definition. Be sure to include sources that students and teachers can act on to enhance readiness because they provide rich information about existing accomplishments and what to focus on to improve.

- Determine the relationship between the definition of college and career readiness and school accountability needs. In other words, which aspects of the definition are most appropriate for schools to be held accountable to address and which are important but may not necessarily lend themselves well to inclusion in an accountability system?

2. *Determine the professional learning, curriculum, and resource supports* schools and educators need in order to provide a high-quality, personalized education for students that can enable college and career readiness.

- Consider which opportunity-to-learn and educational process measures are needed to enable attainment of the outcome measures.

Developing a plan to undertake the changes that may be needed in school funding systems, curriculum frameworks, and professional development supports—and launching work on these fronts—communicates that the state is serious about taking responsibility for its aspects of accountability.

- Develop, disseminate, and implement comprehensive standards, curricular frameworks, learning progressions, instructional tools and modules, exemplars of student work, and other materials aligned to the college and career readiness goals that support classroom practices designed to advance deeper learning outcomes.

- Develop teacher education and development standards and programs that enable educators to learn these practices.

- Support schools in developing approaches that offer all students opportunities to learn the new content in ways that can help them develop deeper learning skills and all teachers opportunities to learn to teach to new standards. Consider the ways in which changes in the use of time and technologies may factor into these new approaches.

3. *Establish a clear framework for a comprehensive system of assessments* aligned with college and career ready outcomes.

- Assess the various ways in which information and accountability needs could be met by a variety of measures, including performance assessments, and integrate measures appropriately into curriculum development and professional learning opportunities.

- Ensure that these include opportunities for teachers to design, score, and discuss rich assessments of student learning.

- Consider how measures could be triangulated, in other words, how information from more than one source could be combined to reach a more accurate or complete judgment about a particular aspect of performance. Many important metacognitive learning skills, for example, can best be measured both as processes and products.

- Create a system of multiple measures for uses of assessments that result in decisions about students, educators, or schools. Where cut scores are proposed or may have been used, identify supplemental data that can be considered in a multiple measures system. Develop profiles of information for evaluating and conveying insights about students and schools.

4. *Work with postsecondary and workforce representatives* when developing these new systems to ensure acceptance of the measures and how they will be used to ascertain and facilitate of college and career readiness.

- Determine beforehand how data from the system could be used by postsecondary institutions and employers and develop safeguards to avoid misuse of data, particularly cut scores.
- Define with postsecondary stakeholders how the results of rich measures of student learning can be best conveyed and used (e.g., digital portfolios; summary data supplemented by a taxonomy of work samples) and what kinds of profiles of information about students will be most useful and usable.

5. *Develop means for system learning* to support continuous improvement at all levels of the system.

- Involve educators in the development and scoring of assessments so that they deeply learn the standards and have opportunities to share practice.
- Document best practices and disseminate knowledge through online platforms sharing studies and highlighting exemplars; school study visits; conferences focused on the sharing and development of practices; feedback loops to students, educators, and schools about their work (e.g., through exhibitions, educator evaluation systems, and school quality reviews); and collaboration opportunities within and across schools and networks.

Research and experience make it clear that educational systems that can accomplish the deeper learning goals now before us must incorporate assessments that honor and reflect those goals. Continued use of high-quality standards and performance assessments has been shown to improve teaching and learning. And as teachers become more expert about teaching, student progress can be expected to follow. Not only can overall pedagogical capacity be enhanced, but assessment can stay focused on its central purpose: the support of learning for all involved. In these ways, new systems of assessment, connected to appropriate resources, learning opportunities, and productive visions of accountability, can provide a critical element in enabling students to meet the challenges that face them in twenty-first-century college and careers.

NOTES

Chapter 1: Beyond the Bubble Test

1. See http://www.corestandards.org
2. Lyman, P., & Varian, H. R. (2003). *How much information*. School of Information Management and Systems, University of California, Berkeley. Retrieved from http://www.sims.berkeley.edu/how-much-info-2003/
3. McCain, T., & Jukes, I. (2001). *Windows on the future: Education in the age of technology*. Thousand Oaks, CA: Corwin Press.
4. Ng, P. T. (2008). Educational reform in Singapore: From quantity to quality. *Education Research on Policy and Practice, 7*, 5–15.
5. Silva, E. (2008). *Measuring the skills of the 21st century*. Washington, DC: Education Sector, p. 5.
6. These states included Connecticut, Kentucky, Maine, Maryland, Nebraska, New Hampshire, New Jersey, New York, Oregon, Vermont, Rhode Island, Washington, Wisconsin, and Wyoming, among others.
7. For a review, see Darling-Hammond, L., & Rustique-Forrester, E. (2005). The consequences of student testing for teaching and teacher quality. In J. Herman & E. Haertel (Eds.), *The uses and misuses of data in accountability testing* (pp. 289–319). Malden, MA: Blackwell.
8. Newmann, F. M., Marks, H. M., & Gamoran, A. (1995) Authentic pedagogy: Standards that boost performance. *American Journal of Education, 104*(4), 280–312; Lee, V. E., Smith, J. B., & Croninger, R. G. (1995, Fall). Another look at high school restructuring: More evidence that it improves student achievement and more insight into why. In *Issues in Restructuring Schools* (Issue Report no. 9, pp. 1–9). Madison: Center on the Organization and Restructuring of Schools, University of Wisconsin.
9. No Child Left Behind Act of 2001 (sec. 1111 B2c(1)). Retrieved from http://www2ed.gov/policy/elsec/leg/esear02/pg2.html
10. US General Accountability Office. (2009). *No Child Left Behind Act: Enhancements in the Department of Education's review process could improve*

113

state academic assessments (Report GAO-09-911). Washington, DC: US Government Accountability Office, p. 20.

11. Yuan, K., & Le, V. (2012). *Estimating the percentage of students who were tested on cognitively demanding items through the state achievement tests.* Santa Monica, CA: RAND.

12. Webb, N. L. (2002). *Depth-of-knowledge levels for four content areas.* Retrieved from http://facstaff.wcer.wisc.edu/normw/All%20content%20areas%20%20 DOK%20levels%2032802.doc

13. Polikoff, M. S., Porter, A. C., & Smithson, J. (2011). How well aligned are state assessments of student achievement with state content standards? *American Educational Research Journal, 48*(4), 965–995.

14. Shepard, L. A. (1996). *Measuring achievement: What does it mean to test for robust understandings?* (William H. Angoff Memorial Lecture Series): Princeton, NJ: Educational Testing Services.

15. Shepard, L. A. (2008). Commentary on the National Mathematics Advisory Panel recommendations on assessment. *Educational Researcher, 37*(9), 602–609.

16. Stecher, B. (2010). *Performance assessment in an era of standards-based educational accountability.* Stanford, CA: Stanford University, Stanford Center for Opportunity Policy in Education.

17. Madaus, G. F., West, M. M., Harmon, M. C., Lomax, R. G., & Viator, K. A. (1992). *The influence of testing on teaching math and science in grades 4–12* (SPA8954759). Chestnut Hill, MA: Boston College, Center for the Study of Testing, Evaluation, and Educational Policy.

18. Jones, B. D., & Egley, R. J. (2004). Voices from the frontlines: Teachers' perceptions of high-stakes testing. *Education Policy Analysis Archives, 12*(39). Retrieved from http://epaa.asu.edu/epaa/v12n39/; Pedulla, J. J., Abrams, L. M., Madaus, G. F., Russell, M. K., Ramos, M. A., & Miao, J. (2003). *Perceived effects of state-mandated testing programs on teaching and learning: Findings from a national survey of teachers.* Boston, MA: Boston College, National Board on Testing and Public Policy; Woody, E., Buttles, M., Kafka, J., Park, S., & Russell, J. (2004). *Voices from the field: Educators respond to accountability.* Berkeley: Policy Analysis for California Education, University of California, Berkeley.

19. Achieve. (2004). *Do graduation tests measure up? A closer look at state high school exit exams: Executive summary.* Washington, DC: Author.

20. See, for example, Snow, C. (2002). *Reading for understanding: Toward an R&D program in reading.* Santa Monica, CA: Science and Technology Policy Institute, RAND.

21. McMurrer, J. (2007). *Choices, changes, and challenges: Curriculum and instruction in the NCLB era.* Washington, DC: Center for Education Policy.

22. Haney, W. (2000). The myth of the Texas miracle in education. *Education Policy Analysis Archives, 8*(41), pt. 6, p. 10. Retrieved from http://epaa.asu.edu/epaa/v8n41/

23. Southeast Center for Teacher Quality. (2004). High-stakes accountability in California: A view from the teacher's desk. *Teaching Quality Research Matters, 12,* 1–2. Retrieved from: http://www.teachingquality.org/ResearchMatters/issues/2004/issue12-Aug2004.pdf, p. 15

24. Schmidt, W. H., Wang, H. C., & McKnight, C. (2005). Curriculum coherence: An examination of U.S. mathematics and science content standards from an international perspective. *Journal of Curriculum Studies, 37*(5), 525–559.

25. Organization for Economic Cooperation and Development (OECD). (2012). *PISA 2-2012 results in focus: What 15-year olds know and what they can do with what they know.* Paris: OECD.

26. Gordon Commission on Future Assessment in Education. (2013). *A public policy statement.* Princeton, NJ: Educational Testing Service, p. 7.

27. Herman, J. L., & Linn, R. L. (2013). *On the road to assessing deeper learning: The status of Smarter Balanced and PARCC assessment consortia* (CRESST Report No. 823). Los Angeles: University of California, National Center for Research on Evaluation, Standards, and Student Testing.

Chapter 2: Defining Performance Assessment

1. Madaus, G. F., & O'Dwyer, L. M. (1999). A short history of performance assessment. *Phi Delta Kappan, 80,* 688–695.

2. Bloom, B. (1956). *Taxonomy of educational objectives, Handbook 1: Cognitive domain.* White Plains, NY: Longman.

3. Madaus, G. F., West, M. M., Harmon, M. C., Lomax, R. G., & Viator, K. A. (1992). *The influence of testing on teaching math and science in grades 4–12* (SPA8954759). Chestnut Hill, MA: Boston College, Center for the Study of Testing, Evaluation, and Educational Policy; Lomax, R. G., West, M. M., Harmon, M. C., Viator, K. A., & Madaus, G. F. (1995). The impact of mandated standardized testing on minority students. *Journal of Negro Education, 64*(2), 171–185.

4. Pecheone, R. L., & Kahl, S. (2010). *Developing performance assessments: Lessons learned.* Stanford: Stanford University, Stanford Center for Opportunity Policy in Education.

5. Hong Kong Educational Assessment Authority. (2009). *School-based assessment: Changing the assessment culture.* Retrieved from http://www.hkeaa.edu.hk/en/hkdse/School_based_Assessment/SBA/

6. The Assessment Continuum was developed by L. Darling-Hammond (2013) for the Stanford Center for Assessment, Learning, and Equity (Stanford, CA).

7. Pecheone & Kahl. (2010).

8. International Baccalaureate Organization. (2005, November). IB *Diploma Programme: English A1, higher level, paper 2*. Retrieved from http://www.ibo.org/diploma/curriculum/examples/samplepapers/documents/gp1_englisha1hl2.pdf

9. Bennett, R. E., Persky, H., Weiss, A. R., & Jenkins, F. (2007). *Problem solving in technology-rich environments: A report from the NAEP Technology-Based Assessment Project* (NCES 2007-466). Washington, DC: National Center for Education Statistics, US Department of Education. Retrieved from http://nces.ed.gov/pubsearch/pubsinfo.asp?pubid=2007466, p. 41

10. Bennett et al. (2007). p. 46.

11. Summarized using information from the Ohio Department of Education Ohio Performance Assessment Pilot Program website: http://www.ode.state.oh.us/GD/Templates/Pages/ODE/ODEDetail.aspx?page=3&TopicRelationID=9&ContentID=61383&Content=78805

12. These include schools working with the Center for Collaborative Education in Boston, the New York Performance Standards Consortium, the International High School Network, New Tech High Schools, Envision Schools, the Met Schools, and others.

Chapter 3: Experiences with Performance Assessment in the United States and Abroad

1. Finnish Matriculation Examination. (2008). Retrieved from http://www.ylioppilastutkinto.fi/en/index.html

2. Singapore Examinations and Assessment Board. (n.d.). *Science Investigations Instructions*. Author.

3. Ng, P. T. (2008). Educational reform in Singapore: From quantity to quality. *Education Research on Policy and Practice, 7*, 5–15, p. 6.

4. Hong Kong Educational Assessment Authority. (2009). *School-based assessment: Changing the assessment culture*. Retrieved from http://www.hkeaa.edu.hk/en/hkdse/School_based_Assessment/SBA/

Chapter 4: How Performance Assessment Can Support Student and Teacher Learning

1. For a summary, see Darling-Hammond, L., & Rustique-Forrester, E. (2005). The consequences of student testing for teaching and teacher quality. In J. Herman & E. Haertel (Eds.), *The uses and misuses of data in accountability testing* (pp. 289–319). Malden, MA: Blackwell.

2. Chapman, C. (1991, June). *What have we learned from writing assessment that can be applied to performance assessment?* Presentation at ECS/CDE Alternative Assessment Conference, Breckenbridge, CO; Herman, J. L., Klein, D.C.D., Heath, T. M., & Wakai, S. T. (1995). *A first look: Are claims for alternative*

assessment holding up? (CSE Technical Report). Los Angeles: UCLA National Center for Research on Evaluation, Standards, and Student Testing; Koretz, D., Mitchell, K. J., Barron, S. I., & Keith, S. (1996). *Final report: Perceived effects of the Maryland school performance assessment program* (CSE Technical Report). Los Angeles: UCLA National Center for Research on Evaluation, Standards, and Student Testing; Stecher, B. M., Barron, S., Kaganoff, T., & Goodwin, J. (1998). *The effects of standards-based assessment on classroom practices: Results of the 1996–97 RAND survey of Kentucky teachers of mathematics and writing* (CSE Technical Report). Los Angeles: UCLA National Center for Research on Evaluation, Standards, and Student Testing; Firestone, W. A., Mayrowetz, D., & Fairman, J. (1998, Summer). Performance-based assessment and instructional change: The effects of testing in Maine and Maryland. *Educational Evaluation and Policy Analysis, 20,* 95–113; Lane, S., Stone, C. A., Parke, C. S., Hansen, M. A., & Cerrillo, T. L. (2000, April). *Consequential evidence for MSPAP from the teacher, principal and student perspective.* Paper presented at the annual meeting of the National Council on Measurement in Education, New Orleans, LA; Koretz, D., Stetcher, B., & Deibert, E. (1992). *The Vermont portfolio program: Interim report on implementation and impact, 1991–92 school year.* Santa Monica, CA: RAND; Stecher, B., Baron, S., Chun, T., & Ross, K. (2000). *The effects of the Washington state education reform on schools and classroom* (CSE Technical Report). Los Angeles: UCLA National Center for Research on Evaluation, Standards, and Student Testing; Darling-Hammond & Rustique-Forrester. (2005).

3. Frederiksen, J., & Collins, A. (1989). A systems approach to educational testing. *Educational Researcher, 18*(9), 27–32; National Council on Education Standards and Testing. (1992). *Raising standards for American education: A report to Congress, the secretary of education, the National Education Goals Panel, and the American people.* Washington, DC: US Government Printing Office, Superintendent of Documents; Resnick, L. B., & Resnick, D. P. (1982). Assessing the thinking curriculum: New tools for educational reform. In B. G. Gifford & M. C. O'Conner (Eds.). *Changing assessment: Alternative views of aptitude, achievement and instruction* (pp. 37–55). Boston: Kluwer Academic.

4. Lane, S., Parke, C. S., & Stone, C. A. (2002). The impact of a state performance-based assessment and accountability program on mathematics instruction and student learning: Evidence from survey data and school performance. *Educational Assessment, 8*(4), 279–315; Stecher, B., Barron, S., Chun, T., & Ross, K. (2000, August). *The effects of the Washington state education reform in schools and classrooms* (CSE Technical Report 525). Los Angeles: UCLA National Center for Research on Evaluation, Standards and Student Testing; Stein, M. K., & Lane, S. (1996). Instructional tasks and the development of student capacity to think and reason: An analysis of the relationship between

teaching and learning in a reform mathematics project. *Educational Research and Evaluation, 2*(1), 50–80; Stone, C. A., & Lane, S. (2003). Consequences of a state accountability program: Examining relationships between school performance gains and teacher, student, and school variables. *Applied Measurement in Education, 16*(1), 1–26.

5. Newmann, F. M., Marks, H. M., & Gamoran, A. (1996). Authentic pedagogy and student performance. *American Journal of Education, 104*(8), 280–312.

6. Lane et al. (2002); Parke, C. S., Lane, S., & Stone, C. A. (2006). Impact of a state performance assessment program in reading and writing. *Educational Research and Evaluation, 12*(3), 239–269; Stone & Lane. (2003).

7. Linn, R. L., Baker, E. L., & Betebenner, D. W. (2002). Accountability systems: Implications of requirements of the No Child Left Behind Act of 2001. *Educational Researcher, 31*(6), 3–16.

8. Borko, H., Elliott, R., & Uchiyama, K. (2002). Professional development: A key to Kentucky's educational reform effort. *Teaching and Teacher Education, 18*, 969–987; Falk, B., & Ort, S. (1998). Sitting down to score: Teacher learning through assessment. *Phi Delta Kappan, 80*(1), 59–64; Darling-Hammond, L. (2004). Standards, accountability, and school reform. *Teachers College Record, 106*(6), 1047–1085; Sheingold, K., Heller, J. I., & Paulukonis, S. T. (1995). *Actively seeking evidence: Teacher change through assessment development* (Report MS No. 94–04). Princeton, NJ: Educational Testing Service; Wolf, S., Borko, H., McIver, M., & Elliott, R. (1999). *"No excuses": School reform efforts in exemplary schools of Kentucky* (Technical Report No. 514). Los Angeles, CA: UCLA, Center for Research on Evaluation, Student Standards, and Testing.

9. Darling-Hammond, L., & Falk, B. (2013). *Teacher learning through assessment: How student performance assessments support teacher learning.* Washington, DC: Center for American Progress.

10. Darling-Hammond, L. (2010). *Performance counts: Assessment systems that support high-quality learning.* Washington, DC: Council of Chief State School Officers.

11. Resnick, L. (1995). Standards for education. In D. Ravitch (Ed.), *Debating the future of American standards.* Washington, DC: Brookings Institution, p. 113.

12. Falk & Ort. (1998).

13. Darling-Hammond, L., & Wood, G. (2008). *Assessment for the 21st century: Using performance assessments to measure student learning more effectively.* Washington, DC: Forum for Education and Democracy.

14. Abedi, J., & Herman, J. L. (2010). Assessing English language learners' opportunity to learn mathematics: Issues and limitations. *Teachers College Record, 112*(3), 723–746.

15. Foster, D., Noyce, P., & Spiegel, S. (2007). When assessment guides instruction: Silicon Valley's Mathematics Assessment Collaborative. *Assessing Mathematical Proficiency, 53*, 137–154, p. 141.

16. Paek, P. L., & Foster, D. (2012). *Improved mathematical teaching practices and student learning using complex performance assessment tasks.* Paper presented at the annual meeting of the National Council on Measurement in Education, Vancouver, Canada.

17. Paek & Foster. (2012).

18. Wei, R. C., Schultz, S. E., & Pecheone, R. (2012). *Performance assessments for learning: The next generation of state assessments.* Stanford, CA: Stanford Center for Assessment, Learning, and Equity, p. 45.

19. Personal communication from William Hart, assistant superintendent, Pentucket Regional School District, Massachusetts, November 6, 2012.

20. Personal communication from Hart.

21. Unless noted otherwise, quotations in this section were retrieved from http://www.qualityperformanceassessment.org/mission/testimonials-and-clients/

22. Personal communication from Laurie Gagnon, director of the Quality Performance Assessment initiative, December 17, 2012.

23. Personal communication from Jeanne Sturgess, staff developer, Souhegan High School, Amherst, New Hampshire.

24. Personal communication from Christina Brown, director of the Quality Performance Assessment's Principal Residency Network, October 23, 2012.

25. Personal communication from Amy Woods, eighth-grade English teacher, Cape Cod Lighthouse Charter School, East Harwich, Massachusetts.

26. Personal communication from Priti Johari, redesign administrator, Chelsea High School, Massachusetts, November 14, 2012.

27. Personal communication from Johari.

28. Foster et al. (2007). pp. 152–153.

Chapter 5: Meeting the Challenges of Performance Assessments

1. Koretz, D., Mitchell, K. J., Barron, S. I., & Keith, S. (1996). *Final report: Perceived effects of the Maryland school performance assessment program* (CSE Technical Report). Los Angeles, CA: UCLA National Center for Research on Evaluation, Standards, and Student Testing.

2. Measured Progress. (2009). *Commonwealth Accountability and Testing System: 2007–08 technical report.* Version 1.2. Retrieved from http://www.education.ky.gov/KDE/Administrative+Resources/Testing+and+Reporting+/Kentucky+School+Testing+System/Accountability+System/Technical+Manual+2008.htm

3. This section relies heavily on Suzanne Lane's paper developed for this project: Lane, S. (2010). *Performance assessment: The state of the art.* Stanford, CA: Stanford University, Stanford Center for Opportunity Policy in Education.

4. Lane, S., & Stone, C. A. (2006). Performance assessments. In B. Brennan (Ed.), *Educational Measurement.* Westport, CT: American Council on Education and Praeger.

5. Baker, E. L. (2007). Model-based assessments to support learning and accountability: The evolution of CRESST's research on multiple-purpose measures. *Educational Assessment, 12*(3&4), 179–194.

6. Lane & Stone. (2006).

7. Lane, S. (2011). Issues in the design and scoring of performance assessments that assess complex thinking skills. In G. Schraw (Ed.), *Assessment of higher order thinking skills.* Charlotte, NC: Information Age Publishing.

8. Niemi, D., Wang, J., Steinberg, D. H., Baker, E. L., & Wang, H. (2007). Instructional sensitivity of a complex language arts performance assessment. *Educational Assessment, 12*(3&4), 215–238, p. 199.

9. Chi, M.T.H., Glaser, R., & Farr, M. J. (Eds.). (1988). *The nature of expertise.* Hillsdale, NJ: Erlbaum; Ericsson, K. A., & Simon, H. A. (1984). *Protocol analysis: Verbal reports as data.* Cambridge, MA: MIT Press.

10. See, for example, Measured Progress. (2009); Collegiate Learning Assessment (2010). *CLA: Returning to learning.* Retrieved from http://www.collegiatelearningassessment.org/

11. Lane. (2011).

12. Collegiate Learning Assessment. (2010).

13. Bennett, R. E., Persky, H., Weiss, A. R., & Jenkins, F. (2007). *Problem solving in technology-rich environments: A report from the NAEP Technology-Based Assessment Project* (NCES 2007–466). Washington, DC: National Center for Education Statistics, US Department of Education. Retrieved from http://nces.ed.gov/pubsearch/pubsinfo.asp?pubid=2007466; Deane, P. (2006). Strategies for evidence identification through linguistic assessment of textual responses. In D. M. Williamson, R. J. Mislevy, & I. I. Bejar (Eds.), *Automated scoring of complex tasks in computer-based testing* (pp. 313–362). Mahwah, NJ: Erlbaum.

14. Klein, S., Benjamin, R., Shavelson, R., & Bolus, R. (2007). The collegiate learning assessment: Facts and fantasies. *Evaluation Review, 31*(5), 415–439.

15. Mislevy, R. (1993). Foundations of a new test theory. In N. Frederiksen, R. Mislevy, & I. Bejar (Eds.), *Test theory for a new generation of tests* (pp. 19–40). Hillsdale, NJ: Erlbaum.

16. Shepard, L. (2005). Assessment. In L. Darling-Hammond & J. Bransford (Eds.), *Preparing teachers for a changing world: What teachers should learn and be able to do.* San Francisco, CA: Jossey-Bass.

17. Wilson, M. R., & Bertenthal, M. W. (2006). *Systems for state science assessment.* Washington, DC: National Academy Press. For a description of England's Assessing Pupils' Progress program, see Darling-Hammond, L., & Wentworth, V. (2010). *Benchmarking learning systems: Student performance assessment in international context.* Stanford, CA: Stanford University, Stanford Center for Opportunity Policy in Education.

18. Kane, M. T. (2006). Validation. In B. Brennan (Ed.), *Educational measurement*. Westport, CT: American Council on Education & Praeger; Messick, S. (1989). Validity. In R. L. Linn (Ed.), *Educational measurement* (3rd ed., pp. 13–104). New York: American Council on Education and Macmillan.

19. Messick, S. (1994). The interplay of evidence and consequences in the validation of performance assessments. *Educational Researcher, 23*(2), 13–23.

20. Foote, M. (2007). Keeping accountability systems accountable. *Phi Delta Kappan, 88*, 359–363; Foote, M. (2012). Freedom from high stakes testing: A formula for small schools success. In M. Hantzopoulos & A. R. Tyner-Mullings (Eds.), *Critical small schools: Beyond privatization in New York City urban education reform*. Charlotte, NC: Information Age Publishing; New York Performance Standards Consortium. (2012). *Educating for the 21st century: Data report on the New York Performance Standards Consortium*. New York: Author.

21. Andrade, H. L., Du, Y., & Wang, X. (2008). Putting rubrics to the test: The effect of a model, criteria generation, and rubric-referenced self-assessment on elementary school students' writing. *Educational Measurement: Issues and Practice, 27*(2), 3–13. See also Barron, B., Schwartz, D. L., Vye, N. J., Moore, A., Petrosino, T., Zech, L., & Bransford, J. D. (1998). Doing with understanding: Lessons from research on problem- and project-based learning. *Journal of Learning Sciences, 7*(3&4), 271–311.

22. Black, P., & Wiliam, D. (1998). Inside the black box: Raising standards through classroom assessment. *Phi Delta Kappan, 80*, 139–148.

23. Darling-Hammond, L., Ancess, J., & Falk, B. (1995). *Authentic assessment in action*. New York: Teachers College Press; Falk, B., & Ort, S. (1997, April). *Sitting down to score: Teacher learning through assessment*. Presentation at the annual meeting of the American Educational Research Association, Chicago; Goldberg, G. L., & Rosewell, B. S. (2000). From perception to practice: The impact of teachers' scoring experience on the performance based instruction and classroom practice. *Educational Assessment, 6*, 257–290; Murnane, R., & Levy, F. (1996). *Teaching the new basic skills*. New York: Free Press.

24. Goldschmidt, P., Martinez, J. F., Niemi, D., & Baker, E. L. (2007). Relationships among measures as empirical evidence of validity: Incorporating multiple indicators of achievement and school context. *Educational Assessment, 12*(3&4), 239–266.

25. Abedi, J. (2010). *Performance assessments for English language learners*. Stanford, CA: Stanford University, Stanford Center for Opportunity Policy in Education.

26. Abedi, J., & Lord, C. (2001). The language factor in mathematics tests. *Applied Measurement in Education, 14*(3), 219–234; Abedi, J., Lord, C., Hofstetter, C., & Baker, E. (2000). Impact of accommodation strategies on English language learners' test performance. *Educational Measurement: Issues and Practice, 19*(3), 16–26.

27. Abedi, J., & Herman, J. L. (2010). Assessing English language learners' opportunity to learn mathematics: Issues and limitations. *Teachers College Record*, *112*(3), 723–746.

28. Goldberg, G. L., & Roswell, B. S. (2001). Are multiple measures meaningful? Lessons from a statewide performance assessment. *Applied Measurement in Education*, *14*, 125–150; Lane. (2010).

29. Delaware Department of Education. (2005). *Text-based writing item sampler*. Retrieved from http://www.doe.k12.de.us/AAB/files/Grade%208%20 TBW%20-%20Greaseaters.pdf, p. 5.

30. Bennett, R. E., Persky, H., Weiss, A. R., & Jenkins, F. (2007). *Problem solving in technology-rich environments: A report from the NAEP Technology-Based Assessment Project* (NCES 2007–466). Washington, DC: National Center for Education Statistics, US Department of Education. Retrieved from http:// nces.ed.gov/pubsearch/pubsinfo.asp?pubid=2007466

31. Vendlinski, T. P., Baker, E. L., & Niemi, D. (2008). *Templates and objects in authoring problem-solving assessments* (CRESST Technical Report 735). Los Angeles: University of California, National Center Research on Evaluation, Standards, and Student Testing.

32. Bennett et al. (2007).

33. Bennett, R. E. (2006). Moving the field forward: Some thoughts on validity and automated scoring. In D. M. Williamson, R. J. Mislevy, & I. I. Behar (Eds.), *Automated scoring of complex tasks in computer-based testing* (pp. 403–412). Hillside, NJ: Erlbaum; Bennett, R. E., & Gitomer, D. H. (2009). Transforming K-12 Assessment: Integrating accountability testing, formative assessment and professional support. In C. Wyatt-Smith & J. Cumming (Eds.), *Educational assessment in the 21st century*. New York: Springer.

34. Pecheone, R. L., & Kahl, S. (2010). *Developing performance assessments: Lessons learned*. Stanford: Stanford University, Stanford Center for Opportunity Policy in Education.

Chapter 6: Making High-Quality Assessment Affordable

1. The College Board charged $89 per subject in 2013 for its Advanced Placement exam. See http://www.collegeboard.com/student/testing/ap/cal_fees.html. In 2012, each subject test for the International Baccalaureate (IB) program cost $104, plus a one-time registration fee of $151. See http://www.mpsaz.org /westwood/academics/ib/parent_group/files/ib_exam_fees.pdf. IB does not publish test prices on its website; however, multiple school websites, including this one, provide identical figures.

2. Chingos, M. (2012). *Strength in numbers: State spending on K–12 assessment systems*. Washington, DC: Brookings Institution; Topol, B., Olson, J., Roeber, E., & Hennon, P. (2013). *Getting to higher-quality assessments: Evaluating*

costs, benefits, and investment strategies. Stanford, CA: Stanford University, Stanford Center for Opportunity Policy in Education.

3. Topol et al. (2013).

4. All calculations of the cost in 2009 dollars were made using the CPI calculator available from the US Bureau of Labor Statistics at http://data.bls.gov/cgi-bin/cpicalc.pl

5. For a review, see Picus, L., Adamson, F., Montague, W., & Owens, M. (2010). *A new conceptual framework for analyzing the costs of performance assessment.* Stanford, CA: Stanford University, Stanford Center for Opportunity Policy in Education. See also US General Accounting Office. (1993). *Student extent and expenditures, with cost estimates for a national examination* (Report GAO/PEMD-93-8). Washington, DC: Author.

6. US GAO. (1993); Stecher, B. (1995). *The cost of performance assessment in science: The RAND perspective.* Presentation at the annual conference of the National Council on Measurement in Education, San Francisco.

7. Table adapted from Hardy, R. A. (1995). Examining the costs of performance assessment. *Applied Measurement in Education, 8*(2), 121–134.

8. Topol, B., Olson, J., & Roeber, E. (2010). *The cost of new higher-quality assessments: A comprehensive analysis of the potential costs for future state assessments.* Stanford, CA: Stanford Center for Opportunity Policy in Education.

9. Feuer, M. J. (2008). Future directions for educational accountability: Notes for a political economy of measurement. In K. E. Ryan & L. A. Shepard (Eds.), *The future of test-based educational accountability.* New York: Routledge; Picus et al. (2010); Darling-Hammond, L., & Rustique-Forrester, E. (2005). The consequences of student testing for teaching and teacher quality. In J. Herman & E. Haertel (Eds.), *The uses and misuses of data in accountability testing* (pp. 289–319). Malden, MA: Blackwell.

10. McLaughlin, M. (2005). Listening and learning from the field: Tales of policy implementation and situated practice. In A. Lieberman (Ed.), *The roots of educational change* (pp. 58–72). New York, NY: Teachers College Press, p. 60.

11. For a recent review of professional development offerings and effectiveness, see Wei, R. C., Darling-Hammond, L., Andree, A., Richardson, N., & Orphanos, S. (2009). *Professional learning in the learning profession: A status report on teacher development in the United States and abroad.* Dallas, TX: National Staff Development Council and Stanford, CA: Stanford Center for Opportunity Policy in Education.

12. Odden, A., Goertz, M., Goetz, M., Archibald, S., Gross, B., Weiss, M., & Mangan, M. T. (2008). The cost of instructional improvement: Resource allocation in schools using comprehensive strategies to change classroom practice. *Journal of Education Finance, 33*(4), 381–405, p. 399.

Chapter 7: Building Systems of Assessment

1. New Hampshire Department of Education. (2013). *Enriching New Hampshire's assessment and accountability systems through the Quality Performance Assessment Framework*. Author, p. 9. Retrieved from http://www.education. nh.gov/assessment-systems/documents/executive-summary.pdf

2. American Educational Research Association, American Psychological Association, & National Council on Measurement in Education. (1999). *Standards for educational and psychological testing*. Washington, DC: American Educational Research Association.

3. Darling-Hammond, L. (1992–93, Winter). Creating standards of practice and delivery for learner-centered schools. *Stanford Law and Policy Review*, *4*, 37–52.

INDEX

A

Abedi, J., 67, 68–69, 70

Accessibility: accountability for, 104; for student subgroups, 47, 67–71. *See also* English Language Learners (ELLs)

Accountability: in assessment systems, 101, 102; capacity building and, 109–111; high-stakes testing and, 75; systems of, 103–105

Achieve, 6

Achievement outcomes, 4, 44, 52

"Acid Rain Task," 32–34

Advanced Placement program, 9, 14, 61, 75, 122*n*.6:1

Alberta, Canada, 62

A-level exams, 28

Analytic skills: assessment of, 90; defined, 17; in mathematics performance task, 27

Application of knowledge and skills: failure to test, 7; need for, in twenty-first century, 3; performance assessment for, 16, 43; US *versus* international performance in, 8

Artificial intelligence, 73, 77

Assessment: broader view of, 6; consequences of, 66–67; continuum of, 19–29; cost-benefit perspective on, 83–86, 107–108; costs of, 75–86; critical objectives for, 9–10; emerging opportunities for better, 9–14; for high-stakes decisions, 5–6; influence of, on learning, 3–8; twenty-first-century needs for, 1–3; in United States *versus* other countries, 8, 18

Assessment Solutions Group (ASG), cost models of, 79–83

Assessment systems: accountability and, 101, 102, 103–105, 109–111; affordability of high-quality, 75–86; approach to creating, 99–103, 109–111; building, 87–105, 109–111; capacity building for, 73–74, 109–111; components of, 88–92; computer-based, 72–73; continuum of assessment options in, 19–29, 79–83; cost-benefit perspective on, 83–86, 107–108; cost-reduction strategies for, 81–83, 85, 108; costs of, 75–86; international examples of, 91–93; New Hampshire's, 100–102; overview of, 87–88; planning, 99–103, 109–111; Queensland's, 91–94; relative emphasis on summative and formative assessments in, 102–103; scope of, 87–88; stakeholders of, 87, 88–89, 99–100, 111; state development of, 99–103; state examples of, 89–91; student guidance and support from, 95–99; teachers' role in, 93–95. *See also* Large-scale performance assessment; State assessment systems

Auditing, of performance tasks and scores, 62, 73, 74, 94, 102

Australia: assessment systems in, 91–93; Developmental Assessment program, 64–65; Queensland, 62–63, 91–94; Victoria, 37–39

Automated scoring, 63, 81. *See also* Computer-based assessment

B

Baron, J. B., 78

Benchmarks: international, 1, 9; for scoring, 46, 62, 63, 74

Best practices dissemination, 111

Biology exam, high school, 37–38

Black, P., 66

Bloom, B., 17

Bloom's taxonomy, 17–18

Breland, H. M., 78
Brown, C., 52
Bubble test. *See* Multiple-choice tests

C

Calibration, 46, 61, 62–63, 72–73
California: performance assessments in, 4, 43, 44, 48–49, 78; teacher comments from, 48–49
California Assessment Program, 78
Camp, R., 78
Canada, Alberta, 62
Cape Cod Lighthouse Charter School, East Harwich, Massachusetts, 53–54
Career readiness. *See* College and career readiness
CCSS. *See* Common Core State Standards
Center for Collaborative Education, 116*n*.2:12
Center on Education Policy, 6–7
Certificates of Initial and Advanced Mastery, 90
Chelsea High School, Massachusetts, 54
China, 63
Classroom-based performance assessments: in assessment systems, 89, 90; combined with centralized assessments, 35, 36–41, 90, 91–92; controlled, 36–37; in high-achieving nations, 35, 36–41, 45; for student learning opportunities, 44–45; for transferable skills, 41
Cognitive demand: of consortia assessments, 10; levels of, 4–5, 17–19; taxonomy based on, 4–5
Cognitive skills, taxonomy of, 17–19. *See also* Higher-order skills
Collaboration, educator, 52, 54, 73. *See also* Teacher discussions
Collaboration skills, 88
College admissions: multiple assessment data needed by, 89, 99, 100; student profiles for, 96–98, 111; tests for, 97
College and career readiness: beyond Common Core State Standards, 13; Common Core State Standards for, 1, 13, 87–88; competencies for, 13; defining, 109; in state assessment systems, 101; student profiles for, 96–98, 111; twenty-first-century needs for, 1–3; in United States *versus* other countries, 8
College and Work Ready Assessment, 23
College Board, 78, 122*n*.6:1
Collegiate Learning Assessment (CLA), 23–24, 63
Common Core State Standards (CCSS): consortia assessments for, 10–13, 81, 83;

emerging assessments for, 9–14; goal of, 1; limitations of, 13; standards of, that cannot be measured by consortia assessments, 87–88; teacher learning about, 53
Communication skills, 88
Computer navigation system, 73
Computer-based assessment: correlations of human-based assessment and, 63; cost reduction through use of, 81, 85; efficiencies of, 72–73; fairness of, 73; reliability of, 73; scoring in, 63, 72–73
Connecticut, 32–34, 43, 78, 90
Connecticut Assessment of Educational Progress, 78
Consequences, of assessment, 66–67
Consequential validity, 66–67
Consortia exams: for CCSS assessment, 10–14, 81, 83; complementary assessments to, 13–14; cost reduction through use of, 81, 83, 85; limitations of, 13, 87–88; for science standards, 9; standards not measured by, 87–88; in student profiles, 97
Construct irrelevant variance, 59
Constructed-response items: cognitive demand differences in, 18–19; defined, 17; with hands-on inquiry tasks, 22–23; types of, 21–22
Context, in performance task, 67
Continuous improvement, 111
Continuous inquiry and improvement, 53
Continuum of assessments, 19–29; assessment options in, 21–29; graphical depiction of, 20; item costs in, compared, 79–83; student role changes in, 19–20. *See also* Assessment systems
Contractor costs, 83
Cost-benefit perspective, 83–86, 107–108
Costs: Assessment Solutions Group (ASG) models of, 79–83; of assessments, 75–86; cost-benefit perspective on, 84–86, 107–108; of high-quality assessments (HQAs), 77–83; of multiple-choice tests, 75–77; of multiple-choice tests compared to performance assessments, 79–83; of open-ended assessments, 75; opportunity, 83–84; strategies for reducing, 81–83, 85, 108; variables in, 77–79
Council for Aid to Education, 23
Council of Chief State School Officers (CCSSO), 13

CPI calculator, 123*n*.4
Critique an Argument performance task, 23–24
Culminating projects, 28–29
Culture of inquiry, 51–54
Curriculum: impact of high-stakes testing on, 6–8; narrowing of the, 6–7; performance task alignment with, 59; rushing through the, 7
Curriculum-embedded performance tasks, examples of, 25–26
Cut scores, 98–99, 110–111

D
Delaware state assessment, 71–72
Diagnostic use, of performance assessments, 45, 70, 107
"Disaster in the Gulf Project," 27–28
Distractor choices, 68
Double scoring, 63
Driving test, 15–16, 43

E
Economies of scale, 77, 79
Educational Testing Service (ETS), 9, 72
Efficiencies: with computer technology, 72–73; cost-reduction strategies and, 81–83, 85, 108; in task design, 71–72
Employers, assessment data needed by, 89, 100, 111
England, 36–37, 64, 91
English Language Arts performance tasks: of Delaware, 71–72; of England's General Certificate of Secondary Education (GCSE), 37; of Ohio Performance Assessment Project, 25; of Partnership for Assessment of Readiness for College and Careers, 12; of Smarter Balanced Assessment Consortium, 12
English Language Arts tests, US spending on, 75
English Language Learners (ELLs): ensuring fairness for, 67–71; linguistic modification for, 59, 68–71; task piloting for, 60, 70–71
Envision Schools, 116*n*.2:12
"Evaluating Amelia Earhart's Life" performance task, 12
Evaluation skills, 17
Evidence-based teaching, 47, 51
Examinations boards, 62, 91

Expenditures: diminishing per capita, for high-quality assessments (HQA), 82; on US testing, 75–77, 123*n*.4. *See also* Costs
Explanation task, 59–60
External moderators, 62, 94

F
Factory skills, 2
Fairness, 47, 67–71, 73
Families, 99–100
Feasibility, 71–74
Federal accountability, 104–105
Field testing, 60–61
Financial aid decisions, 99
Finland, 35–36
Formative assessments: in assessment systems, 88, 102–103; computer-based, 72; as guidance for students, 95–96; positive consequences of, 66

G
Gagnon, L., 51
General Accountability Office (GAO), 4
General Accounting Office, 77
General Certificate of Secondary Education (GCSE), 36–37, 91
Geometry proofs, 78
"Golf Balls in Water" performance task, 11
Gordon Commission on Future Assessment in Education, 9–10
Grade point average, 97
Graduation decisions, 99
Graduation portfolios, 28–29, 32, 90–91
Growth, measuring, 63–65. *See also* Learning progressions

H
Hands-on inquiry tasks, 22–23
Hawaii, 59–60
"Heating Degrees Task," 26
Helium gas balloons, simulation task, 22–23
Herman, J. L., 10
High-achieving nations: assessment systems of, 91–93; cost-benefit perspective and, 84; deeper coverage in, 8; examples of, 34–41; external testing in, 35–36; higher-order skill assessment in, 18; performance assessments in, 8, 34–41, 45

Higher-order skills: consortia assessments of, 10–14; failure to assess, in current US tests, 4–8, 18; high-achieving nations' assessment of, 34–41; performance assessments as support for teaching, 50–51; taxonomies of, 4–5, 17–18; testing, concepts of, 17–19; in United States *versus* other countries, 18

High-stakes assessment: cost-benefit perspective on, 83–86, 107–108; decisions made from, 5–6, 98–99; expenditures for, 75–77; problems with, 5–6, 98–99; reliability for, 58–59

Hill, R., 78

History tests, 21, 32

Hong Kong, 19, 63

Hybrid assessment model, 22

I

Illinois, 16–17

In-basket approach, 23–24

Industrial economy, 2

Innovation Lab Network, 13–14

Inquiry, culture of, 51–54

Inquiry standard, 90

Institute for Learning, University of Pittsburgh, 46

Instruction: coherence in, 51–54; influence of high-stakes testing on, 6–8

Instructional improvement: cost-benefit perspective and, 84–86; through evidence, 47, 51; performance assessment as support for, 9, 43–55; through teacher involvement in scoring, 46–45, 66

Interdisciplinary projects, 39–41

International Baccalaureate exam: costs of, 75, 122*n*.6:1; performance assessments in, 9, 14, 21–22, 28; score calibration in, 63

International competitiveness, 1, 3

International examples. *See* High-achieving nations

International reform, 3

International standards, 1, 9

International High School Network, 116*n*.2:12

Interrater reliability, 61–63. *See also* Reliability

Issue analysis, 90

J

Johari, P., 53

Jones, R. J., 78

Juried exhibitions, 28, 116*n*.2:12

K

Kentucky: performance assessments in, 4, 32, 43, 44, 73, 74; scoring costs in, 78; writing portfolio of, 32, 58, 61

Knowledge, rapid expansion of, 2–3

L

Lane, S., 44, 59–60

Large-scale performance assessment: affordability of, 75–86; in assessment systems, 88–89, 101; capacity building for, 73–74, 109–111; computer-based, 72–73; consistent scoring for, 74; constructed-response tasks in, 21–22; cost-benefit perspective on, 83–86, 107–108; cost-reduction strategies for, 81–83, 85, 108; experiences with, 31–41; feasibility of, supporting, 71–74; field testing, 60–61; in high-achieving nations, 8, 34–41, 91–93; item costs in, compared, 79–83; meeting the challenges of, 57–74; overview of, 14; simulations in, 22–23, 72; states' development of, 99–103; in US, 3–4, 31–34, 89–91

Learning: influence of testing on, 3–8, 44; ways that performance assessment support, 43–55, 95–96. *See also* Student learning; Teacher learning

Learning opportunities. *See* Student learning opportunities

Learning profiles, 90

Learning progressions, 64–65, 72, 92–93

Learning-to-learn skills, 95, 98

Leather, P., 53–54

Levy, F., 2

Licensure examinations, 72

Linguistic modification, 68–71

Linn, R., 44

Local accountability, 104–105

Locally sourced foods project, 27

Lynn, R. L., 10

M

Maine, 4, 31–34, 43, 44, 90

Make an Argument performance task, 23–24

Maryland, 4, 43, 44, 90

Maryland School Performance Assessment Program, 44

Massachusetts, 50–51, 52–53, 73

Math Online Project, 63

Mathematical models, 88

Mathematics Assessment Collaborative, 54–55

Mathematics Assessment Resource Service (MARS), 48–49

Mathematics performance tasks: costs of, 80; for English Language Learners, 59, 67, 68, 69–70; of Finland, 35–36; of Ohio Performance Assessment Project, 26; of Partnership for Assessment of Readiness for College and Careers, 11; of Smarter Balanced Assessment Consortium, 10–11

Mathematics tests, standardized, 18; costs of, 80; US spending on, 76

Matrix sampling, 90

Medicine, computer-based simulations in, 72

Met Schools, 116n.2:12

Minnesota, Profiles of Learning, 90

Mislevy, R., 63

Missouri, 32, 43

Moderation processes, 46, 52–53, 61, 62–63, 94

Morris, M. M., 78

Motivation, student, 97

Multiple-choice tests: in assessment continuum, 19; in assessment systems, 90; cognitive demand of, 4–5; cost-benefit perspective on, 83–86, 107–108; costs of, 75–77; costs of, compared with performance assessments, 79–83; English Language Learners and, 67–68, 70; impact of, on teaching and learning, 6–8; limitations of, 4–6; performance assessments *versus*, 15–17, 67–67; state reliance on, due to No Child Left Behind, 4, 75

Murnane, R., 2

N

National Assessment of Educational Progress (NAEP): achievement outcomes and, 44; automated scoring in, 63; simulation tasks of, 22–23, 63

National Science Foundation, 18

NCLB. *See* No Child Left Behind

Netherlands, 94

New England Common Assessment Program (NECAP), 31–32

New England, Quality Performance Assessment (QPA) initiative in, 50–54

New Hampshire: assessment system plan of, 100–102; large-scale assessment in, 89; performance assessments in, 31–32, 43, 52, 53–54; teacher comments from, 52

New Hampshire Department of Education, 89

New Jersey Special Review Assessments (SRAs), 68, 69–70

New Tech High Schools, 116n.2:12

New York, 43, 73, 74, 90

New York City, teacher comments from, 48

New York Performance Assessment Consortium, 66

New York Performance Standards Consortium, 28–29, 91, 116n.2:12

New York State Regents Examinations: overview of, 74; performance components of, 32; Physics exam, 18–19; scoring of, 62; US history test, 21; waiver option for, 91

Next Generation State Standards (NGSS), 9

No Child Left Behind (NCLB): costs of assessments for, 75, 79–83; goal of, 9; impact of, on instruction, 6–8; impact of, on state assessments, 4–5, 31–32, 57, 91; improving on, 9

"Nuclear Power—Friend or Foe?" performance task, 12

O

Obama, B., 1

Office of Technology Assessment, 78

Ohio: performance assessments in, 25–26, 43; teacher comments from, 49

Ohio Performance Assessment Project, 25–26, 49

On-demand testing: in assessment systems, 90; classroom-embedded supplements to, 36–39; performance components in, 32, 35

Online research skills assessment, 23

Opportunity costs, 83–84

Oregon, Certificates of Initial and Advanced Mastery, 90

P

PARCC. *See* Partnership for Assessment of Readiness for College and Careers (PARCC)

Partnership for Assessment of Readiness for College and Careers (PARCC), 10; costs of, 76; sample performance tasks of, 11, 12

Peer assessments, 95

Pentucket Regional School District, Massachusetts, 50–51

Performance assessment: affordability of, 75–86; benefits of, 43–55, 84–86, 108, 111–112;

cost-benefit perspective on, 83–86, 107–108; cost-reduction strategies for, 81–83, 85, 108; costs of, 77–86; defining, 15–29; emerging opportunities for, 9–14; feasibility of, ways to support, 71–74; as guidance for student learning, 95–99; large-scale, 14; for measuring growth, 63–65; meeting the challenges of, 57–74; *versus* multiple-choice tests, 15–17; rationale for, 1–14; school coherence and, 51–54, 92; for special needs student populations, 67–71; as support for student and teacher learning, 43–55

Performance assessment systems: NCLB impact on, 4–5, 31–32, 34; state, past experiences with, 3–4, 31–34, 43–44, 89–91. *See also* Assessment systems; State assessment systems

Performance measures, 9, 14

Performance tasks: basic form of, 21–22; cognitive demand levels of, 18–19; context in, 67; continuum of, 21–29; design of, 59–60, 71–72; efficiencies in design of, 71–72; fairness of, 67–71, 73; field testing, 60–61, 70–71; forms of, 17; with multiple scores, 71–72; PARCC sample, 11, 12; project types of, 13, 25–29; reliability and validity of, 58–67; reviewing, 60–61; SBAC sample, 10–11, 12; in state assessment system, 101–102; templates for, 59–60; web-based bank of, 102

Physics performance tasks, 16–17, 18–19, 63

"Planning a Field Trip" performance task, 10–11

Policies, accountability, 103–105

Policymakers, 14, 89, 90, 95, 100

Portfolios: in assessment systems, 28–29; deeper learning and, 51; graduation, 28–29, 32, 90–91; reliable scoring of, 43, 58, 61, 94; in state assessment systems, 32, 58; technology, 32, 91

Professional community, teacher, 47, 55

Professional development: cost-benefit perspective on, 85; cost-reduction models of, 74, 81, 82, 83; performance assessment as support for, 44, 46, 54–55; workshop model of, 85

Professional development days, teacher scoring on, 74, 83

Professional development institutes, 102

Professional standards of practice, 104

Profiles, student, 90, 96–98, 111

Program for International Student Assessment (PISA), 8, 19

Program placement decisions, 99

Progress map, 64–65

Projects: complex, 13; continuum of, 25–29; culminating, 28–29; interdisciplinary, in Singapore, 39–41; longer-duration, interdisciplinary, 27–28

Proxy items, 68

Q

Quality Performance Assessment (QPA) initiative, 50–54

Queensland, Australia, 62–63, 91–94

Queensland Curriculum, Assessment, and Reporting Framework (QCAR), 92

R

RAND Corporation, 4–5

Reading ability, 67. *See also* English Language Learners (ELLs)

Reform: in 1990s, 3–4, 43, 44, 57, 115*n*. 2:6; for broader assessment, 6; international, 3; performance assessment as Trojan horse for, 85; twenty-first-century needs for, 1–3

Regional support networks, 102

Reidy, E., 78

Reliability: in computer-based assessments, 73; concerns about, 58–59; methods for ensuring, 46, 59–67, 94

Remediation decisions, 99

Research, extended, 88

Resnick, L., 46

Review, task, 60–61

Rhode Island, 31–32, 43, 90–91

Rich science tasks, 32–34. *See also* Science performance tasks

Rock, D. A., 78

Rubrics, 46; in computer-based assessment, 73; continuity in, 52–53; design of quality, 61–62; task design and, 59

S

SAT, costs of, 78

SBAC. *See* Smarter Balanced Assessment Consortium (SBAC)

School achievement, impact of performance assessments on, 44

School coherence, 51–54, 92

School-level accountability, 104, 109

Science performance tasks: in Connecticut, 32–34; experimental, 32–34; in Hong Kong, 19; in Illinois, 16–17; inquiry-oriented, 22–23; of NAEP, 22–23; New York State Regents, 18–19; in Queensland, Australia, 92–93; in Singapore, 39, 91; in Victoria, Australia, 37–38

Science standards, 9, 16

Science tests, standardized, 18

Scoring: benefits of teacher involvement in, 45–55; collective, 46, 47, 51–54; computer-based, 63, 72–73, 81; costs of, 77–83; ensuring consistency in, 61–63, 74; moderation processes for, 46, 52–53, 61, 62–63, 94; on-site, contractor, 83; portfolio, 43, 58, 61, 94; on professional development days, 74, 83; validity and reliability of, 61–63

Self-assessments, 95

Self-reports, 97

Shanmugaratnam, T., 3

Shepard, L. A., 5

Silicon Valley Mathematics Initiative, 48

Simulation tasks, 22–23, 63, 72

Singapore: assessment system of, 3, 28, 39–41, 91, 94; Examinations and Assessment Board (SEAB), 39–40; Project Work (PW), 39–41

Skill levels: continuum of assessment and, 19–29; taxonomies of, 4–5, 17–19. See also Higher-order skills

Skills. See also Higher-order skills; Twenty-first-century skills

Skills, changed demand for, 132

Smarter Balanced Assessment Consortium (SBAC), 10, 101; costs of, 76, 83; sample performance tasks of, 10–11, 12

Solution strategies, 88

Souhegan High School, Amherst, New Hampshire, 52

Stakeholders: assessment system for multiple, 88–89, 99–100, 111; types of, 87; working with, 111

Standards: internalization of, 66, 74, 95; internationally benchmarked, 1, 9; teaching to, through involvement in scoring, 46, 47, 53–54; twenty-first-century needs for, 1–3. See also Common Core State Standards

Standards for Educational and Psychological Testing, 98

State accountability, 104–105

State assessment systems: of the 1990s, 3–4, 43, 44, 89–91, 115n:6; achievement outcomes of, 4, 44; capacity building for, 73–74, 109–111; development of, considerations for, 99–103, 109–111; examples of, 89–91; high-stakes testing in, 5–6; NCLB's impact on, 4–5, 31–32, 34, 57, 91; skill levels tested in, 4–5. See also Assessment systems; Large-scale performance assessment

Stecher, B., 5

Stevenson, Z., 78

Stipend model, 81, 82, 83

Student learning: in assessment systems, 94–96; consequences of assessment and, 66; deeper, performance assessments as support for, 50–51; feedback as guidance for, 95–96; measuring progressions in, 63–65, 72, 92–93; opportunities for, classroom-embedded performance assessments for, 44–45; understanding individual methods of, 47–49; ways that performance assessment supports, 43–55, 95–96

Student learning opportunities: accountability for, 104, 109–111; classroom-embedded performance assessments for, 45–46; for special needs student populations, 70; supporting schools to provide, 109–111

Student profiles, 90, 96–98, 111

Students: diagnosing, 45, 70, 107; with disabilities, 68; English Language Learner, 59, 60, 67–71; high-stakes decisions about, 98–99; measuring growth and change in, 63–65; motivation of, 97; roles of, in continuum of assessments, 19–20; self-direction in, 66; special needs population, 67–71; as stakeholders of assessment systems, 95–99; traditionally underserved, 9; understanding the thinking of, 47–49, 72, 73, 94

Sturgess, J., 51–52

Summative assessments: in assessment systems, 88, 102–103; computer-based, 72; costs of high-quality (HQA), 79–83

Synthesis skills, defined, 17

System learning, 111

T

Table leaders, 62

Task design: efficiencies in, 71–72; for reliability and validity, 59–60

Task input, routine and nonroutine, 2

Teacher discussions: learning in, 46, 47, 51–54; for score moderation, 62–63, 81, 94

Teacher involvement: in assessment systems, 93–95; benefits of, to student and teacher learning, 43–55, 67, 85; in computer-based assessment, 73; cost-reduction through, 81, 85–86; school coherence and, 51–54

Teacher learning: in assessment systems, 94; consequences of assessment and, 66–67; from involvement in scoring, 45–55, 67, 73; performance assessments as support for, 45–55. *See also* Professional development

Teacher-moderated scoring cost-reduction strategy, 81; professional development model of, 81, 82, 83; stipend model of, 81, 82, 83

Teaching. *See* Instruction

Teaching improvement. *See* Instructional improvement

Teaching to the standards, 46

Teaching to the test, 6

Technological advances, 14, 72–73. *See also* Computer-based assessment

Technology portfolio, 32, 91

Templates, 59–60

Transcripts, 96

Transferable learning: in cost-benefit perspective, 83, 84; as rationale for school-based assessments (SBA), 41

Triangulation, of multiple measures, 96, 110

Twenty-first-century skills: demand for, 2–3; educational changes needed for, 1–3; NCLB impact on, 6–7; performance assessments as support for teaching, 50–51. *See also* Higher-order skills

U

United States: assessment expenditures in, 75–77; score ranking of, *versus* other countries, 8; state performance assessments in, past experiences with, 3–4, 31–34, 43–44, 89–91

US Bureau of Labor Statistics, 123*n*.4

US Congress, 4

US Department of Education, 4, 57

University of California, Berkeley, 2–3

University of Pittsburgh, Institute for Learning, 46

V

Validity: consequential, 66–67; methods for achieving, 58–67, 94

Vermont: performance assessments in, 4, 32, 43, 44, 73, 90; portfolio system of, 58

Victoria, Australia, 37–38

W

Washington State, 4, 44

Webb taxonomy, 4–5

Wiliam, D., 66

Wisconsin, 90

Woods, A., 52–53

Work, changing nature of, 1–3

Writing performance tasks, multiple dimensions assessed in, 71–72

Writing portfolios, 32, 58

Writing tests, constructed-response items in, 21–22, 32

Wyoming, 90